FULL DAYS ON THE LAKELAND FELLS

25 challenging walks in the Lake District

Adrian Dixon

Published by Sigma Leisure – an imprint of
Sigma Press, 1 South Oak Lane, Wilmslow, Cheshire SK9 6AR, England.

British Library Cataloguing in Publication Data
A CIP record for this book is available from the British Library.

ISBN: 1-85058-434-6

Typesetting and Design: Sigma Press, Wilmslow, Cheshire.

Photographs: Adrian Dixon, unless where otherwise stated.

Cover photograph: On Sharp Edge, Blencathra (by Mark Walsh)

Maps: Adrian and Marion Dixon

Printed by: J.W. Arrowsmith Ltd, Bristol

Disclaimer: the information in this book is given in good faith and is believed to be correct at the time of publication. No responsibility is accepted by either the author or publisher for errors or omissions, or for any loss or injury howsoever caused. Only you can judge your own fitness, competence and experience.

Contents

The Walks

Route 22:
When on High Street . . .

Distance: *13¾ miles.*
Total Ascent: *2900ft.*

Route 23:
Blencathra and Beyond

Distance: *10 miles.*
Total Ascent: *2900ft.*

Route 24:
Breaking New Ground behind The Northern Giants

Distance: *12½ miles.*
Total Ascent: *2850ft.*

Route 25:
The 'Seven Threes'

Distance: *47 miles.*
Total Ascent: *10250ft.*

Index of Features Visited

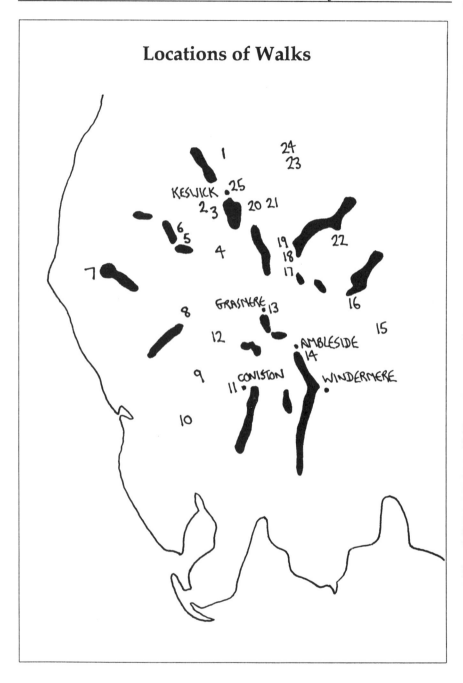

Introduction

Full Days On The Lakeland Fells is the culmination of a long standing desire to put together a collection of walks amongst the high peaks of the Lake District which would present demanding yet attainable challenges. But what exactly constitutes a 'full day'? As we each have our own walking and climbing pace which we regard as comfortable, and spend varying degrees of time on the summits themselves, the phrase really defies definition suffice to say a day amongst the fells is what we as hillwalkers make it.

As a starting point for the length of the routes, I worked on a minimum distance of ten miles as, speaking from personal experience, I always feel a great sense of accomplishment when the mileage gets into double figures. 'Edging Around Helvellyn' is the only one falling just short of this mark, but in my opinion is a route of more than sufficient quality to excuse itself from this particular statistic. As regards the amount of climbing each route should attempt to reach, one figure immediately sprung to mind. It could not really be anything other than three thousand feet; not only because, thanks to Sir Hugh Munro, the figure is revered in the annals of Scottish hillwalking history, but also as far as Lakeland and indeed England is concerned, it represents that very special contour above which so little ground stands. All but three routes make this figure.

You will notice I have not set out specific times for the routes for the reasons outlined above, preferring to use a range instead. As a minimum, I consider the well documented Naismith's Rule of one hour for every three miles, plus an extra half hour for every thousand feet of ascent to be pretty close to the mark, plus an extra third to a half of the above at the outside. These margins should be comfortable for the majority of hillwalkers who have graduated to walks of this type.

So to the routes themselves. The majority are circuits, along with several linear walks, starting in the north of the district, then moving west, south, east and back to the north. Some are well known and hence would be conspicuous by their absence, with others not nearly as acclaimed. By taking advantage of the many magnificent ridges which abound in Lakeland most of the major peaks can be visited without prolonged bouts of descent and resultant re-ascent. This is definitely one advantage Lakeland's fells have over their Scottish compatriots.

As the Lake District National Park covers only 880 square miles, it would be an onerous task to plan a large number of long walks without some degree of overlap. I have no doubts such a task is achievable, however I believe the end result would contain significant unpleasant detours incorporated into the walks simply to avoid covering the same ground more than once. With this in mind, and taking the book as a whole, a handful of summits is therefore visited more than once.

The fells are not there to be climbed just the once and their names ticked off on some sort of 'mountain shopping list'; we should explore them to the full and make use of the network of paths and tracks which enable us to do just this, but we should tread carefully. There are plenty of examples of our carelessness when it comes to path erosion. Sometimes the grassy borders look more inviting to walk on than the muddy track, but such actions only make things worse in the long term as we end up with unsightly scars which blight the landscape. We must learn from our mistakes and learn fast.

The rugged Borrowdale Volcanics and the undulating moorland of the High Street fells on the eastern fringe are classic examples of the variations which exist in what is really a microcosm when compared with the vast tracts of unfrequented territory in Scotland, but nevertheless Lakeland remains a place which holds us in its grip and draws us back again and again. Rather like poring over a map for the umpteenth time, there is always something new to discover when walking in the high ground of the Lake District.

For the statistically minded, nearly all Lakeland's fifty highest peaks, and a total in excess of a hundred and thirty different summits are visited, requiring three hundred and seventy miles of walking and over one hundred thousand feet of climbing.

I could not let this opportunity pass without expressing my sincere thanks to a number of people. To Mark Walsh, with whom I have trod many a mile in researching the routes, for valuable editorial comment and advice; to Jill & Neil Richardson and Sue & Dave Spencer for their input, and to my wife Marion, for transportation with a smile (most of the time), assistance with the maps and, for her tolerance and understanding during the past year whilst these pages were compiled.

Public Transport

Considering the geology of the Lake District National Park, it would be asking a lot for all the routes described to be able to make use of public transport, but it is pleasing to note that (currently) most can. Stagecoach Cumberland (the major bus operator) to their credit have still maintained a good bus service within the district, becoming more frequent during the summer months, when early morning and late afternoon services can give access to big walking days. Cumberland's Explorer ticket which provides unlimited travel in Lakeland on any given day can prove extremely useful, particularly for linear routes, and is excellent value at £4.99 (at the time of writing). The Mountain Goat also runs services to the more remote villages, notably Buttermere. Timings are as ever, subject to change and even cancellation, thus regrettably there can be no guarantees of availability. Up to date timetables are usually readily obtainable from Tourist Information Centres and should always be checked before starting out.

Whilst on the subject of public transport, I would take this opportunity to give a special mention to the Friends of the Lake District, who in Summer 1994 grasped the region's traffic congestion 'nettle' in providing monies for an experimental weekend bus service between Staveley and Kentmere, running four times a day in an attempt to reduce the numbers of vehicles in the valley. The service received a very mixed reception in the local press, but despite this it may well prove to be the shape of things to come.

Bus services detailed in the Walk Files at the beginning of each route are those run by Cumberland, unless otherwise stated.

Maps

The sketch maps which accompany each route are included to give a flavour of what to expect, and as such are by no means intended to be the definitive document for navigation purposes. The accuracy and detail of the maps of the Ordnance Survey (to which the Walk Files exclusively refer) fulfil this function, and knowledge of how to use them, along with a compass, is essential before venturing into the high fells.

Gear

With the exception of the long distance 'Seven Threes' route, where use of fell training shoes may be beneficial, walking boots should be considered the norm on mountain terrain, to give the required support and waterproofing. Outdoor clothing has come a long way as regards technological advances, and as a consequence many excellent garments fill the retailers' stores. Cost may in some cases seem prohibitive, particularly where waterproofs are concerned, but along with boots, this is an important investment, as to keep Lakeland rain at bay, you certainly need something very effective. Fleece jackets, by no means essential, have really caught on as a warm extra layer.

Food

From jam butties to the remnants of the previous night's take away, the hillwalker's packed lunch is an object of mystery, and an intriguing topic of conversation. We all know what we like, but does it serve us well during a strenuous day amongst the fells where around four thousand Calories are required?

The guesthouse 'Full English' is psychologically considered to be a good thing to have to start the day off, an opportunity to get as much hot food inside you as you can. Tasty though it is, fatty food is difficult to digest and is an inefficient energy source. Sugary food and bread are good providers of easier-to-break-down carbohydrate, so the twelve (well it has been paid for) slices of guesthouse toast and marmalade we devour does actually have some benefit.

A demanding walk expends a lot of energy, which needs to be replaced in the shortest possible time. This is where further carbohydrate providers come in, such as nuts or nutty bars, chocolate, cake, bread rolls or sandwiches, fruit, and plenty of liquid. I wouldn't live it down if I didn't include Kendal Mint Cake here, not everyone's preference but useful nonetheless. Although the day's major resting period is the fell-top lunch break, it is wise to take smaller regular breaks to eat and drink to top up the energy reserves being constantly depleted. If tackling a number of challenging routes on consecutive days, evening meals containing pasta, rice or potatoes give a useful carbohydrate store for the following day's events.

Shooting The Fells

As a consequence of hillwalking becoming an extremely popular way to spend leisure time, a specialist branch of photography has evolved. We are today able to appreciate this art form at its very best through the results of skill and technique in the many fine glossy publications which hit the bookshelves with pleasurable regularity. The peak conquering snapshot poses we have all indulged in from time to time will always have their importance in any collection, however with a general understanding of the subject matter and the capabilities of your equipment, you can increase your photographic repertoire to improve the quality of your pictures and achieve consistently good results to be proud of.

Rucksack capacity will invariably dictate the amount of gear you can take, and with the weight factor involved this will need to be kept to a minimum. Safety in the hills is of course paramount, so all items essential for your expedition should take priority over photographic gear. Nevertheless, the camera can usually be squeezed in somewhere.

The Single Lens Reflex (SLR) camera has proved extremely popular due to its durability and flexibility with the facility to interchange lenses easily. Today's SLR market is awash with 'do-it-all' computerised models, which calculate light readings, focus the lens and even wind the film on to the next frame for you after the shutter has been pressed. All very convenient as the majority of shots will turn out fine, however fickle mountain lighting can and does play havoc with metering, necessitating corrective action. In this branch of photography, there will always be a place for manual mode or indeed the fully manual camera, where the user is entirely in control of his own destiny.

If your camera has detachable lenses, careful consideration should be given to the number and type to be used. Focal lengths vary widely, with the standard lens being 50mm. A lens of this length records scenes very close to what the eye sees by way of scale, but sometimes more flexibility is required, which is where the zoom lens comes into its own. This lens covers a range of focal lengths, enabling the user to include more of the overall scene in the frame (wide-angle), or pick out particular detail and remove the peripheral view (telephoto). To cater for the majority of situations in this way, mountain photography does not really call for a huge range of focal lengths, therefore zoom lenses covering 35mm-70mm, or slightly wider ie 28mm-80mm, are ideal. Lens hoods prevent incidental light from entering the lens, reducing the chance of flare.

As there will invariably be a number of features in the frame at different distances from the camera, a large depth of field is essential if the whole scene is to be focused. This is achieved by using small apertures, signified by big f-numbers such as f22. Conversely, wider apertures (small f-numbers) give a narrow depth of field with only part of the overall scene sharp. The difference between f-numbers is an f-stop. The f-number is that resulting from dividing the lens's focal length by its aperture diameter.

Colour film is used extensively in the hills, with transparencies (slides) giving excellent colour rendition, and are the usual medium for presentations using projector and screen. Colour negative film also produces high quality results. Black and white film tends to be used more these days by the specialist wishing to exhibit his work, but having said this I recommend you experiment with it as monochrome may turn out to be your particular preference.

Film types also vary in terms of their speed. The ISO (International Standards Organisation) number indicates the sensitivity of the film to light. In a nutshell, the faster the film, the larger its light sensitive grains, and as a consequence, results can show a rough texture to them. Slower films contain smaller grains and thus are much better for detail. The most typical film used by the mountain photographer is medium speed (ISO 100), which is of sufficient grain to produce good results for a range of lighting situations, and sufficiently small apertures can normally be used to record large depths of field. The finer grain of slower speeds (down to ISO 25) can also produce good landscapes, but if lighting is not bright, wider apertures may be needed to compensate, reducing the possibilities for large depths of field.

Combined with selective use of filters scenes can be accentuated to create atmospheric, even surreal effects. Two of the most popular filters used in colour photography are the Skylight or Ultra Violet (UV) filter and the Polarising filter. UV filters absorb ultra violet radiation which reduces haze and hence improves clarity. The polarising filter can be an extremely valuable asset, in that it is used to cut down glare from the sky and from water. The filter can be rotated whilst attached to the lens front, and works by blocking polarised light reflected from minute particles in the atmosphere, and enhancing blue skies. To ensure sufficient light reaches the film in balancing the polarising effect, the lens aperture should be opened up by one to one and a half f-stops. Graduated grey filters (with the darker grey bit positioned at the top of the frame) are invaluable when taking pictures directly into the sun.

Black and white landscapes can also benefit greatly from the use of filters, in varying the appearance of their many shades of grey. For example, it can be difficult to reproduce cloud and sky contrast, as the sky commonly turns out lighter on the developed print. A yellow filter corrects this in darkening skies, and red filters darken them further.

A tripod is generally of little use, unless conditions are very calm and it can be satisfactorily stabilised. A small bean bag is useful for sitting the camera on for self timer shots if you're out on your own and you want to get yourself in the picture.

Unpredictable mountain weather does present many opportunities for photography, so be prepared at all times. Spring sees the peaks (occasionally) reappearing from their blanket of snow and ice, revealing superb colour contrasts with the emergence of fresh growth. The last of the snows is usually to be found resisting the thaw, packed hard into gullies and ravines. Although obviously the best temperature wise, Summer is by no means the best month for mountain photography, as extensive haze commonly prevails which proves beyond the most penetrative capabilities of the average filter. As the sun remains high in the sky for most of the day, flat and shadowless lighting results. Early morning and late evening give better situations.

Autumn offers striking colour combinations over the landscape with more effective directional light as the hours of daylight begin to diminish with the onset of clearer air coupled with falling temperatures. The arrival of snow and ice displays magnificent Winter panoramas as the hills assume alpine stature, but can be a photographer's nightmare. Even the most high-tech metering systems can be tricked, as if the sun is out, light will be reflected from everything within the frame. Exposure settings will take account of this and consequently can unwittingly underexpose the snow cover. Some experimentation is called for in such circumstances, and a way of compensating for this underexposure is to open up the aperture an f-stop. By taking a number of shots at different f-stops (bracketing) you are not wasting film, but increasing your chances of getting an acceptable result. After all, you have most likely spent a great deal of time, and expended a great deal of effort, in gaining your preferred vantage point, so why settle for anything less?

'Mountains don't move, therefore they must be easy to photograph' - not so. It is always well worth taking the time to study your subject from a number of angles (not the easiest thing to do when in the hills) to take advantage of cloud formations and shadows and to evaluate its optimum position within the frame. The peak seen slap bang in the middle of the shot is of little interest; try to include someone in the foreground to give an impression of scale. A further tried and tested technique to achieve a balanced picture aesthetically pleasing to the eye is the 'Rule of Thirds'. By using imaginary lines on the viewfinder which divide the scene equally into thirds both vertically and horizontally, the subject is positioned at one of the four intersections of these imaginary lines. By siting other subjects on the diagonally opposite intersection provides balance without an element of symmetry.

Getting good results with the camera in the hills is simply a matter of practice. It is satisfying to be able to walk the high level ridges, and reach their summits, and equally satisfying to be able to look back at a set of prints or slides on which the day has been faithfully captured. Unlike memories, these records do not fade.

Opposite: Looking into Upper Ennerdale from Crag Fell

The Walks

Route 1:
A Wilder Side of Skiddaw

Walk File

Distance: 10¼ miles.

Total Ascent: 3400ft.

Start/Finish: Car Parking area, Orthwaite Road, south of Bassenthwaite village. (GR 236311, OS Landranger Map Sheet 90).

Terrain: Good ridge paths, with some rough walking to Skiddaw. The route becomes less obvious after leaving the Skiddaw House road.

Lakeland Maps: OS 1:50000 Landranger series Sheet 90 Penrith & Keswick. For more detail of the southern section, use OS 1:25000 Outdoor Leisure series NW sheet no.4.

Public Transport: Nothing which is convenient.

Features visited:

Ullock Pike	2230ft
Long Side	2405ft
Carl Side	2447ft
Skiddaw	3054ft
Bakestall	2189ft

According to the purist (or perhaps I should say devil's advocate) the name of Bassenthwaite has become synonymous with the home of the only 'true' lake in the Lake District; it is a place not usually recognised as a convenient base for venturing into the high fells. Nevertheless, only three miles or so from Bassenthwaite village, or 'Bass' as it is locally known, are a number of highly under-rated members of the extensive Skiddaw group, where even in today's busy Lake District, you can still experience solitude away from the throng. In addition, this route offers a great opportunity to uncover a side of the area's highest peak not often seen close up, by way of a magnificent unfrequented ridge.

The start point is a secluded car park on the narrow road to Orthwaite,

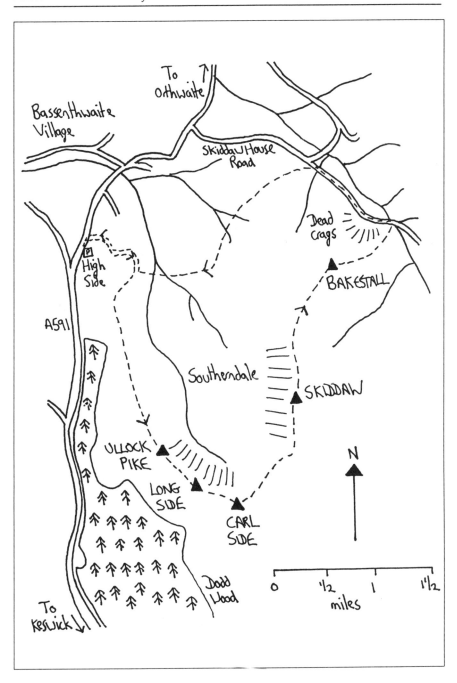

just off the A591 between Keswick and Bassenthwaite. A matter of fifty yards beyond what is really no more than a large passing place, a signpost at a gate points the way, where paths immediately fork left and right. Take the latter and follow a series of distinctive blue arrows nailed to posts and stiles to direct you legitimately through a number of fields, to emerge at the end of the lonely Southerndale valley. A most unusual sight in these early stages is a curiously located seat right on the top of the small hillock to your left. From the Southerndale path, turn sharp right at the gate and stile to accompany the intake wall for a short way in order to gain the beginning of the main ridge.

The narrow and occasionally worn track which starts up from the wall soon merges into the shorter and more popular approach from the Ravenstone Hotel, passing close by one of two close prominent groupings of isolated boulders at around the 1000ft contour. The group you pass is known as the 'Watches', the other a nameless collection which can be viewed across the valley nestling just below the wall on Little Knott. The going underfoot could not really be better, as you climb steadily along the undulating crest of Ullock Pike's gentle northern ridge. The views either side could not be more contrasting; the enormous mass of Skiddaw across the wild recesses of Southerndale to your left, and the verdant Bassenthwaite valley on the right, which is an ornithologist's delight, particularly for wading birds. The heathery flank maintains a very consistent gradient up until the final couple of hundred feet, when the angle of ascent becomes much tougher, yielding a small peaked top at 2230ft above steep slopes. Ullock Pike is an excellent place from which to appraise the open northward sweep of the Solway coastline backed by the hills of southern Scotland.

The ridge now begins to trend east of south now accompanied by a clear track which sticks to the highest ground. Impressive views are plentiful as you proceed along this crest above steepening terrain. This short section is known as Longside Edge, and is appropriately named for the next prominent rise you encounter has with the passage of time gained recognition as Long Side summit, at 2405ft. Somewhat disparagingly referred to as a mere 'Mound' on the 2½" OS map, a second fine viewpoint marked by a carefully constructed cairn now lies at your feet, and only a matter of minutes after the panorama from Ullock Pike. The thin ridge track never strays too far from the sharp northern declivity, but to follow its line conscientiously will actually lead to an unwanted traverse of the northern flank of your next intended peak, Carl Side, instead of attaining its summit. In good conditions, once a small area of level ground is reached on leaving Long Side, it is safe to veer slightly right and strike directly across the grassy shoulder for the short ascent to the highest ground. A variation route is available to you should you so decide, in continuing the aforementioned ridge to Carlside Col and its small tarn, to then almost double back on yourself in order to hit the summit from the northeast via a short steeper climb. Neither is difficult. A pile of stones crown the top at 2447ft at the head of the Southerndale valley and is the greatest elevation reached thus far, but not for long as the illustrious 3000ft contour will shortly be breached.

Skiddaw from Derwent Water

With the immense scarred west face of Skiddaw threatening to swallow up Carl Side whole, you will probably agree the highest inches of this satellite peak are sufficiently welcoming to devoting a lunchtime to, with a view to restocking your energy levels for what appears a potentially unpleasant scramble ahead. A distinct track starts up direct from the col and soon enters a huge expanse of slate and stone which litters the vast slope, for a tiring but fortunately straightforward climb of some 800ft before coming up for air at the south end of Skiddaw's long summit crest.

In absolutely appalling weather one Easter weekend several years ago

I was one of a group of four who inadvertently omitted Carl Side's summit completely, but only realising this fact when, 'comfortably' ensconced in Skiddaw's summit shelter nearly an hour later. As you could barely see your hand in front of your face amidst lashing rain, nobody fancied a return 'peak bagging' journey, committed though we then were to this contagious activity. I continued to regret this embarrassing oversight for some time as my energies always seemed to be channelled into climbing other hills, but having rectified this situation, I would not recommend Carl Side be ignored, being so tantalisingly near to the blazed trail and a useful place for fully appreciating the enormity of the parent fell.

The walking across the length of Skiddaw's stony top is an enjoyable and usually windswept finish to this excellent line of ascent, which you may be surprised to learn is slightly shorter in terms of mileage when compared with the most used way to the top, namely the 'tourist' path from Keswick, which is trodden by many thousands of determined walkers year in year out. Its main summit at 3054ft, England's fourth highest, is actually the third rise crossed when approaching from the south, and is marked by a weather beaten OS column and stone shelter, whose seating space whatever the weather always seems to be fully booked up by happy smiling visitors well satisfied with their achievements.

As an all round viewpoint Skiddaw is superlative, displaying virtually all Lakeland's main mountain groupings huddled seemingly far below. The fine Ullock Pike to Carl Side ridge is sadly now quite dwarfed in retrospect, with the scene west given considerable depth by the position of the Isle of Man directly behind it.

Just about all who have toiled and sweated to reap the rewards of this revered summit retrace their steps southward for one of the numerous routes of descent on offer. However to continue the circuit you need to break with this convention and instead keep to the ridge to maintain a northerly direction over a fourth and final rise, the north top. Descend gradually to a fence corner, and accompany it for half a mile to the point where it again kinks right for the valley below. From this turning point proceed north across the final easy slopes to arrive at Bakestall's shapely cairn of large rocks at 2189ft, a seldom visited summit overtopping the wild and desolate Dash valley.

Dangerous terrain lurks a short distance to the northeast of Bakestall's bleak top in the form of the unnervingly named Dead Crags, therefore the key to ensuring a safe passage to lower ground is to take the thin track initially heading due east, and never too far from the main fence you parted company with only a short while ago. Keep the fence close by for the walk down to the Dash valley to a gate across the only route for vehicular access into the heart of the Skiddaw Forest to Skiddaw House. This is an important staging post in the 'Back O'Skidda' wilderness. When following this road down, do not miss the opportunity of taking a closer look at the rushing falls of Whitewater Dash which pierce the deafening silence of this stark place, Lakeland at its most unspoilt.

At a further gate where Dead Beck meets the road just above the fork to Dash farm, continue straight ahead keeping the intake wall immediately to your right to follow a long and intermittent track to round the joint northern flanks of the subsidiary tops of Cockup and Broad End. These two miles involve a couple of hundred feet of extra climbing, but overall little height is lost thus giving good views over the Bassenthwaite 'flatlands' on the way round to Barkbethdale.

At a corner the wall turns right and the route duly follows it, through bracken and marshy ground down to a large sheepfold, to ultimately rejoin the main path to follow the familiar blue arrows in reverse direction to the car park.

Route 2: A Coledale Collection

Walk File

Distance: 10¼ miles.

Total Ascent: 3600ft.

Start/Finish: Stair, Newlands Hause road.

Terrain: Undulating, generally grassy hills with few steep climbs and good paths the whole way.

Lakeland Maps: OS 1:25000 Outdoor Leisure series NW sheet no.4.

Public Transport: Mountain Goat Bus Keswick – Buttermere. Stops Ellas Crag for Stair.

Features visited:

Causey Pike	2090ft
Scar Crags	2205ft
Sail	2536ft
Crag Hill	2749ft
Grisedale Pike	2593ft

From the approach to Keswick along the A591 your eye always seems to be drawn towards the disordered assortment of the Coledale Fells which form the backdrop to Derwent Water. Cramped into what is actually quite a confined space there are over a dozen peaks and among them a number of mouth watering natural ridge routes await the tempted hillwalker. Five of the best summits of the group can be easily linked together presenting a fine route on high level terrain which remains above 2000ft for nearly its whole distance. Unlike the Fairfield and Kentmere 'horseshoe' walks which have become recognised as classics over the years, a circuit among the Coledale fells does not readily spring to mind. This is a great shame, for this route certainly ranks as one of the finest Lakeland has to offer.

The starting point is on the minor road just above the hamlet of Stair, situated at the western edge of the Newlands valley approximately three miles from Keswick. It is worth remembering that here there are very

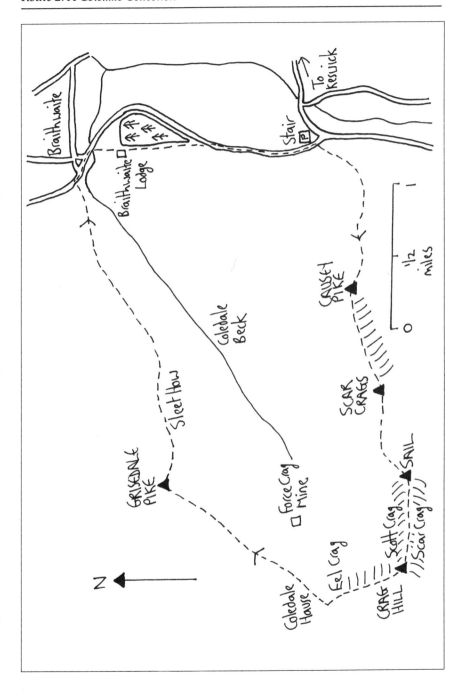

few car parking spaces therefore an early start is highly recommended, but take care not to block off the farm access road in the rush to get started.

From the roadside the distinctive peak of Causey Pike dominates the scene, with its rippled summit ridge beckoning the fell enthusiast. The climbing is immediate and several stone steps ease the first few yards, but you already have a dilemma to solve as two paths are available. One inclines gradually up the eastern flank, with the other striking directly up the steep heathery slope of Rowling End, the large eastern protuberance of the Pike. I'm sure you will not be able to resist the attraction of the latter.

Causey Pike from Newlands

After surmounting Rowling End, the path continues westwards along Sleet Hause, and is met by the easier track at a plateau on the short ridge before the climb to the summit. The path attacks the rocky defences directly, making no real attempt to find an easier line, so forge ahead and enjoy the short scramble to the summit at 2090ft. From the valley floor you will be already aware there is much more to this top, but this approach has concealed its true length; the summit ripples stretch away for surprisingly quite some distance. The view from the cairn is as extensive as any to be found in the district, and well worth taking the time to savour.

Causey Pike is one of those fells which is instantly recognisable from afar and its shapely outline as seen from Friar's Crag on Derwent Water is regarded as one of the Lake District's most outstanding scenes undoubtedly featuring in the collections of many keen photographers. Be warned, as a Causey Pike 'summiteer', you are probably being immortalised on film in your moment of achievement.

The way ahead lies directly over the ripples on a good path which follows the crest of the ridge, and after some twenty minutes you will arrive at the flat crown of Scar Crags. Being in the company of more illustrious neighbours, it is perhaps the least remembered of today's quintet, but then I suppose one of them has to have that dubious honour. I however will always remember it as providing me with my first opportunity to put my then new ice axe into use on the high fells. Snow conditions that day several years ago were nothing short of perfect, with the winter sun casting fans of light onto the slopes through broken cloud – an exhilarating experience not to be forgotten.

Scar Crags stands at 2205ft, and is normally used as a brief halt before proceeding to Sail and the 2500ft contour. Continue generally southwestwards down to the intervening col of Sail Pass. The depression provides a route of escape to Buttermere, Newlands and the Coledale valley itself. The ridge ahead of you is broad and easy, climbing a reasonable gradient to the summit of Sail at 2536ft. Considering its size, the small top although generally devoid of striking features, is worthy of greater recognition than its simple cairn of a handful of rocks. Maybe somebody will do something about this one day. A short distance from the cairn to the north there is a tremendous bird's eye view of Force Crag mine, sitting snugly beneath the crag of the same name in the upper Coledale valley.

Zinc and lead were initially mined at Force Crag from the 1830s through to the early 20th Century. At the end of the First World War the price of metals fell sharply and this led to a change in product to Barytes. Force Crag continued to be worked by enthusiasts, eventually closing in 1991 as the last bastion of mining activity in the Lake District.

Rejoin the main ridge for the short ascent which passes above Scott Crag and Scar Crag in order to reach the highest point of the day, Crag Hill, at 2749ft. Unlike the previous three, this summit is very broad and covered with shattered pieces of slate. Accurate navigation in mist is also vital, for as its name suggests, crags are never too far away. The main features to look out for here are the OS column and a small summit 'shelter' which looks like the only surviving section of a wall which has long since disappeared. All the same, what remains still offers welcome respite from the wind which this expansive top seems to attract. The views are also exceptional, particularly southwards revealing a large number of Lakeland's highest fells.

From the summit, two routes of descent are available. The clear path to the west heads for Grasmoor, and is that which is usually followed, but there is a more exciting alternative. Cross the summit plateau in a northwesterly direction before scrabbling down on rough scree close by Eel Crag (the name sometimes given to the fell itself). This more direct route terminates at Coledale Hause, with the huge flank just descended towering high above.

The scree and rock now give way to grassy slopes for the easy north-east walk to Grisedale Pike, passing close by an old mine shaft of Force Crag, now fenced off for safety reasons. After traversing an un-named subsidiary summit on the main ridge, indicated only by its spot height on the 2½" OS map, follow the ruined wall which runs up the easy side of Grisedale Pike to the summit cairn at 2593ft. This too is slate covered, and also an outstanding vantage point, despite the fact that it turns out to be nothing like as peaked a top as it appears from a distance. The retrospective view along the ridge displays the precipitous face of Hob-carton Crag, with an extensive sweep of north west Cumbria and the Solway Firth with Criffel on the horizon. It is also interesting to retrace your steps (metaphorically speaking of course) back around to Causey Pike which is most impressive in profile.

A couple of years ago, I was engaged in a summit conversation with a chap wearing a kilt. I feel sure he cannot have been forewarned of the reputation Grisedale Pike has for being one of the more windy summits, otherwise he may have donned alternative clothing. Fortunately no offending gusts manifested themselves on that occasion, therefore he was spared the ultimate embarrassment of inadvertently revealing to a sassenach the answer to that age old question of just exactly what is worn under that historic garment.

The first 500ft of the descent (Sleet How) is quite steep and rocky, requiring the use of steadying hands in places to avoid mishaps. Once you are past this section, the terrain becomes much more conducive to making rapid progress and it is very tempting to take to your heels in true fell running fashion down the final ridge. The path traverses the undulating slopes of Kinn before petering out into a wide but steepish grassy sward indented with a staircase of boot prints which have been rigourously used over the years and thus have mitigated the effects of erosion. If anyone wanted evidence of what can be achieved if we took care of where we walked then I cannot think of a better example.

A number of large welcoming boulders amongst the bracken are conveniently located at the foot of this slope and I would recommend you take advantage of them and let your joints recover from what is a knee jarring descent. Cross the fence via a stile and continue down the track which becomes a superbly constructed series of wood-abutted steps cut into the fell-side which certainly make the going much easier over the steep ground. The steps lead out into a small car park which is usually full to overflowing, to the extent that vehicles are left on the grass verge on the Whinlatter Pass roadside nearby.

It is always desirable to avoid road walking wherever possible, as however short the stretch of tarmac it always seems to succeed in draining away any last reserves of energy you may have managed to retain. Here, unfortunately, it cannot be avoided. The first of two short sections which thankfully is all downhill will eventually bring you to Braithwaite village. From the village follow the Newlands road for a short distance, leaving it to the right at a cattle grid in the direction of Braithwaite Lodge. A slate sign fixed to the solitary yew tree in front of the house indicates the way through the farm buildings. Climb the stile immediately ahead to pick up the good path which keeps above a small plantation before meeting up with the Newlands road a short way from your start point at Stair. If you've done this walk with a companion, you could always spin a coin to see who tramps the final section from Braithwaite to fetch the car – but dare you run the risk of losing?

Route 3:
The Grand Tour of Newlands

Walk File

Distance: 15¼ miles.

Total Ascent: 5000ft.

Start/Finish: Hawes End.

Terrain: Good paths and tracks along distinct ridges.

Lakeland Maps: OS 1:25000 Outdoor Leisure series NW sheet no.4.

Public Transport: Nothing which is convenient.

Features visited:

Catbells	1481ft
Maiden Moor	1887ft
High Spy	2143ft
Dale Head	2473ft
Hindscarth	2385ft
Robinson	2417ft
Knott Rigg	1791ft
Ard Crags	1906ft

When it comes to Lakeland valleys, we each have our own personal favourites. Although deeply subjective, up amongst the front runners is sure to be Newlands, which still today remains unspoilt and uncommercialised. Those who hold the valley in high regard, including myself, can savour a number of very fine short walks amongst the fields, farms and hamlets, all well worth taking a closer look at and not just on rainy days. In marked contrast to this pastoral scene, steep and rocky slopes rise sharply throughout the length of the valley floor, and this rather non-standard circuit explores their outer ridges in an eight peak day amongst splendid walking territory.

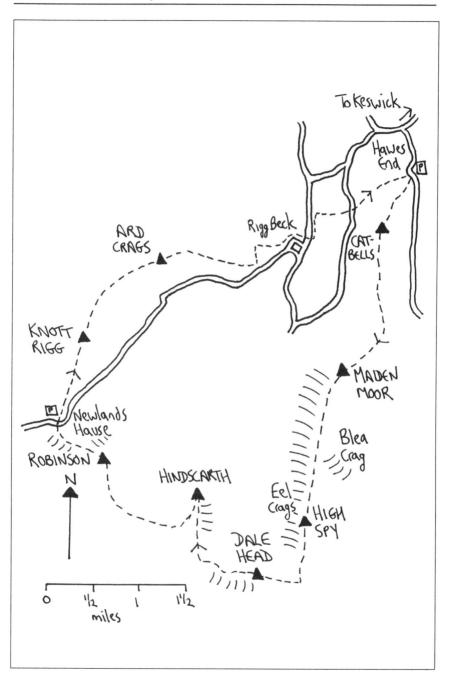

Start from Hawes End at the foot of Catbells, one of Lakeland's most popular short climbs. At weekends many cars line the approach road to the open fell; more parking can be found in a small area beyond the cattle grid alongside the narrow road to Skelgill.

To begin with, Catbells' lower slopes are steep, however enormous volumes of eager visitors have created a well worn groove in the hillside over the years, which considerably aids progress. As you will discover to your consternation, the first 'top' gained on the ridge only reveals the main summit beyond a depression, but the going throughout this ascent never proves difficult including the last few feet on rock, and before you know it Catbells will be beneath your feet. Measuring only 1481ft, the fell can only be described as modest, a word which by no means befits the view from the tiny rugged summit in the midst of a magnificent montage of many mountains.

After Catbells, an easy descent follows to Hause Gate, the meeting place of two well used ways onto the ridge out of both Newlands and Borrowdale. Craggy ground becomes increasingly prevalent on both sides of the path, which maintains a safe line by swinging southwest-ward. Where the path splits continue right, above Bull Crag to cross Maiden Moor's flat top. A simple cairn stands at 1887ft, only one of a number of fine viewpoints from the expansive summit.

Shortly after departing in the direction of High Spy, Maiden Moor's two paths are reunited, continuing as one across Narrow Moor, with the isolated promontory of Blea Crag only a short way off the beaten track to the left. A succession of crags begin to assemble westward, giving High Spy a quite formidable appearance when observed from the Newlands valley, but above them the walking is easy to the large cairn at 2143ft, thoughtfully its base accommodating a few seating places. A short stroll to the edge of the escarpment opens up dramatic aerial views of Newlands.

Although Dale Head, your next peak, is clearly visible in the near distance, the continuation of High Spy's crags force you still further southward involving a significant loss of hard earned height. Cross Newlands Beck at Rigg Head, the turning point of this short section, for a brief reascent up to Dalehead Tarn. Last time I was here on a still warm September morning a couple of young sheepdogs were being put through their paces; the piercing whistles and cries of their handlers reverberating eerily amongst the outcrops of Dale Head's considerable eastern flank.

From the reedy tarn a distinct track can be seen striking up the slope at its right edge. Here is a superbly constructed path of inlaid rock, making an anticipated slog much more pleasurable, whilst keeping a safe distance from dangerous ground to the right. The 2½" OS map reveals one buttress having taken the name of one such Great Gable, which seems to automatically give it enhanced status amongst its neighbours.

The last couple of hundred of feet leaves the made path behind, and continues on rough terrain before arrival at Dale Head itself, at 2473ft the highest point of the round, and possessing a summit cairn which commands attention. Here is a well-fashioned stone structure which appears to defy the laws of gravity, such is its teetering proximity to a steep plunge into the valley it presides over. Breathtaking views are all around you, with no finer place for admiring the contrasting beauty of the wilds

The summit of Dale Head

of upper Newlands leading out to green and fertile pastureland.

Next on the list is Hindscarth. Set back some way from the main ridge, it is the most aloof of the trio of high fells which combine to make up a formidable northern wall above the road to Honister Pass. A good path leaves the summit to take the line of the ridge, with Pillar resplendent in the distance to the southwest and the tremendous rock-face of Honister Crag seen at its very best immediately to your left. Only a small number of iron fence posts now accompany the rough descent of Hindscarth Edge to a 'cairn' of a handful of rocks and a small post indicating the beginning of the diversion along the short, almost perpendicular ridge to Hindscarth. Aloof the hill may be, but its approach path is well beaten out and makes for untroubled walking.

By adding a few more strides beyond the highest point at 2385ft, you will reach a high walled stone shelter and in doing so, bring the rest of this fine north ridge into view, sweeping down into the valley over Scope End. This top is very much a poor relation in terms of height when compared with the parent fell, however when seen from the valley bottom the two combine to form a mini-range of slender stand-alone peaks; a most imposing sight.

The last of the trio is the curiously and simply named Robinson, which lies a further mile west across Little Dale. To reach it, some retracing of steps is necessary, branching right in order to descend to a small col via an erosion stricken trench. A good path by a guiding fence then begins the climb of Robinson, leaving the fence right at a big pile of stones for a short stroll across the flat grassy top to attain the summit cairn at 2417ft, sitting atop the largest of a number of rock outcrops. Among fell-runners Robinson is well known, as it is the first peak (or last if you go clockwise) on what must be the ultimate in Lakeland 'walks', the Bob Graham Round. To gain membership of this elite club, 72 miles must be walked and an incredible 27,000ft climbed to visit 42 peaks, all within 24 hours. Imagine climbing almost the height of Everest from sea level in a day and you have what is required of you if you are to emulate the feats of Mr Graham. I can only dream on.

In departing Robinson you should pick up a sketchy but cairned track to the northwest. This keeps above Moss Beck, but then aims straight for the horrendous bog of Buttermere Moss. To therefore avoid a thorough soaking, traverse further left to join the path along the side of the Moss which does not guarantee dry feet, but does pass through much less of the morass. An awkward little descent through a scree filled cleft then follows, to bring you to the road at Newlands Hause. This loss of over a thousand feet is unavoidable as you cross the road to a much shorter ridge of only two fells hemmed in by higher neighbours on either side.

Knott Rigg is the first of the two. A footpath sign indicates an obvious way ahead, on an improving track up the grassy incline, with a false summit opening up the undulating ridge. Some boggy ground is met towards the meagre summit cairn at 1791ft, but certainly not enough to spoil your enjoyment of the final approach, offering impressive views of Wandope and Eel Crag across a classic V shaped valley. After six exacting tops, this walk measures every inch of its one map mile from the roadside.

Maintain the crest for a further mile to the second prominent rise in the shape of Ard Crags. After two depressions on an ever improving path and a spectacular view down onto the rooftops of Keskadale Farm, the highest point at 1906ft is gained.

With all eight peaks now behind you, it is Rigg Beck you should now aim for, and the continuation of the ridge sweeps down through heather and bracken, surmounting the knoll of Aikin Knott in the process. The path meets a wall (private land beyond) therefore a change of course is compulsory down to the beck, which has to be crossed via stepping stones to pick up the prominent path cutting through the hills from Buttermere. This leads gradually down to a quaint stone bridge at a loop in the valley road near a large house (unusual for its purple colour).

A short road walk brings you to a gate on the right just beyond Emerald Bank where a footpath leads through trees to Rowling End farm beneath Causey Pike. A further gate provides access through fields, to the footbridge over Newlands Beck and on to a lower valley road, for Little Town. A hundred yards up ahead to the left in the direction of Catbells is a signpost for Skelgill, reached via a number of stiles. Follow the permitted way through the farm buildings up to the Catbells 'fell road' back to the cattle grid, finally returning to Hawes End.

Route 4:
Borrowdale's Forgotten Fells

Walk File

Distance: 12½ miles.

Total Ascent: 3400ft.

Start/Finish: Small parking area, near Stonethwaite village.

Terrain: A challenge to route finding in places, with indistinct tracks and a pathless climb. Rough ground and grassy traverses are encountered.

Lakeland Maps: OS 1:25000 Outdoor Leisure series NW sheet no.4 and SW sheet no. 6.

Public Transport: Bus service 79 (The Borrowdale Bus) Keswick – Seatoller.

Features visited:

Rosthwaite Fell	1807ft
Glaramara	2560ft
Allen Crags	2572ft
Sergeant's Crag	1873ft
Eagle Crag	1650ft

The Borrowdale valley is endowed with an abundance of excellent routes into the high fells, most of which situated at its southern end with Seatoller and Seathwaite both extremely favoured starting points. The tract of rugged high ground which rears up very impressively immediately beyond the village of Rosthwaite is more often than not appreciated from through the window of the car or bus on the way to the valley's end, and its fells looked down upon from the greater heights of the Scafell/Gable groups. This route, one of Borrowdale's least frequented, proves an interesting round above the desolate Langstrath valley. Here are quiet fells which there is every chance you could have to yourself, yet strangely are located only a stone's throw from Lakeland's most populous hillwalking territory.

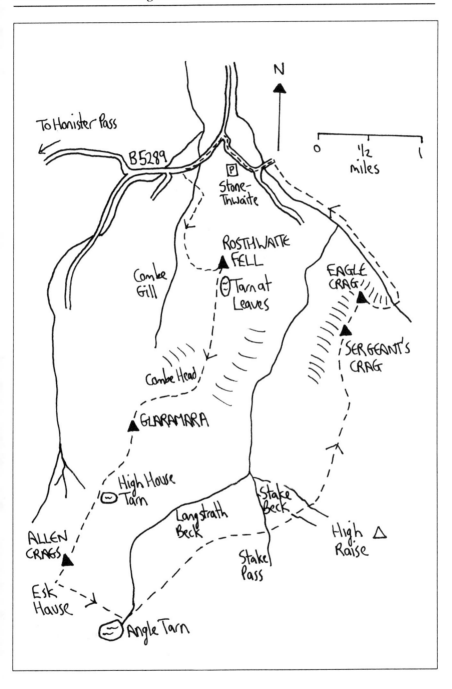

The car can be left in a small area part way down the road to Stoneth-waite off the B5289. If using the Borrowdale Bus from Keswick, you can alight at the aptly named terraced houses of Mountain View and return from the Stonethwaite road junction. Just before the houses a gate at a public footpath signpost (GR 253137 on the 2½" OS map, NW sheet) opens up access through fields to a small bridge over Combe Gill. A second gate leads to a wide track, but this is not a public right of way – a waymarking arrow indicates the beginning of the climb by a line of cairns up to a distinct stony track which heads off to the right through bracken above the gill's tumbling falls, and in so doing contouring the lower slopes of your first target, Rosthwaite Fell. At a large sheepfold beyond a further gate, bear left up the steep flank which at once becomes an interesting test in picking the optimum line amongst an inestimable number of rocks.

This arduous scramble is only short lived in that you soon emerge at a small hollow from where a good track blazes a southward trail. After only a short distance along this track, the up to now concealed Tarn at Leaves appears, set in a secluded dip on this most curious summit expanse. The large rocky knoll up ahead thrusting skyward is Rosthwaite Cam, one of the fell's many 'tops', but not the true summit, although from this point you would be forgiven for thinking a feature of such stature should be. From the tarn, the summit lies back to the north but requires no more than a short detour on a sketchy track up to the highest point at 1807ft, affectionately known as Bessyboot.

Rosthwaite Fell stands at the northern end of a complicated and undulating chain of three fells, which proceeds to gain height gradually, and is one of a number of ridges radiating from the well known hub of Esk Hause. The next two miles to your next fell, Glaramara, is arguably the most intriguing ridge walk you will come across anywhere in Lakeland. It begins simply enough with the retracing of steps back to Tarn at Leaves, then continues along the good path on its west side. So far so good. Very soon the knobbly terrain forces the route to take a convoluted course in a desperate attempt to find a line of least resistance, and in doing so the ever thinner path does become difficult to make out at times, accompanied by only the occasional directional cairn.

After passing a handful of tarns in a small patch of marshy ground by Combe Head, one of the better used routes to the fell is joined, climbing out of the Borrowdale valley via Thornythwaite Fell. Now a much clearer path can be picked up beneath a short rock-face which contains an easy but sporting little scrabble to at long last gain Glaramara's summit. A number of cairns can be found up here, with the path leading directly to the main one, at 2560ft. This summit is very close to the centre of the Lakeland fells and therefore offers extremely good views in all directions, with many peaks to spot.

On your way to the third and final summit of this ridge, Allen Crags, for more fine views you should make a point of detouring only slightly to the other main cairn which is clearly visible a couple of hundred yards southwest, and only negligibly lower than the first. On rejoining the ridge path, a twisting descent follows to the first of several small boggy hollows where lines of stepping stones ensure momentum is maintained. Beyond Lincomb Tarns and High House Tarn (this is a very watery ridge) the route does begin to make its mark on the landscape in the shape of a rougher path which with cairns alongside, winds up the last rocky 100ft of Allen Crags to its ample cairn at 2572ft. To the southwest the precipitous crags of Great End and the eroded Scafell Pike 'motorway' are clearly in view, with the opposite way a fine mountain sweep. Next stop

North from Allen Crags

the Esk Hause wall shelter, but not before lunch at this commanding location – you're more likely to be able to get a seat up here.

The width of the path dropping down to this best known of hillwalking crossroads along the short southern flank of Allen Crags provides sufficient evidence of the fell being taken advantage of, regularly 'bagged' by way of a quick 'there and back' detour. It seems those with only the most dogged determination continue beyond Allen Crags bound for Glaramara.

Once down at the wall shelter, join the Great Langdale – Scafell Pike thoroughfare descending southeastward, the commencement of a long walk between fells. As you would expect from one of the main routes to England's highest mountain, the path is worn, but the gradients turn out to be very easy on the way to Angle Tarn, set in a small hollow flanked by steep crags and a popular resting place for those 'Scafell Piker's' making the tortuous Rossett Gill climb out of the Langdale valley.

Angle Tarn is a significant point on today's route, as in order to gain the eastern rim of the Langstrath valley, the wide path is left to run its course in favour of a narrower track branching left and breasting the northwest slopes of Rossett Pike towards the top of the Stake Pass. The going is quite muddy in places, but the way round to the highest point of the route joining Langdale with Langstrath is clear.

From the pass pick up the path as though dropping down into upper Langstrath, but before too much height is lost, turn east to cross the stream of Stake Beck to gain the huge flank of High Raise. As its summit is not included on the day's agenda, the alternative to a steep and tedious slog calls for a demanding and pathless traverse to reach your next peak, the rocky tor of Sergeant's Crag which can be seen breaking out of the northern landscape in the near distance. Do not aim directly for it as craggy ground bars the way, but forge across the incline crossing several more streams in the process to a depression where the slim ridge track from High Raise can be met. A wooden ladder scales a substantial wall, the final obstacle to the summit which has been a long time coming. A big cairn topping a rocky base marks the highest ground at 1873ft.

Sergeant's Crag is sited at the southern end of a barrier of treacherous crags which serve to enhance its status and also that of its near neighbour to the north, Eagle Crag, particularly as neither of the two top the 2000ft contour. The ridge walk between the two presents little difficulty. The path swings east to follow the wall you climbed earlier, eventually re-crossing it where it again changes direction in heading off right. A short rock step near the edge of a steep plunge provides the necessary impetus to get this little bit out of the way with the minimum of fuss.

The summit cairn is now easily attained. If you thought Sergeant's Crag's top was impressive this one is even better, a small pile of stones at 1650ft perched at the very edge of a sloping rock slab far above Langstrath, which is very well seen, coupled with a spectacular bird's eye view over Stonethwaite.

Eagle Crag's craggy northern face is better left well alone as a way down, therefore a preferred way back to Stonethwaite is to head back for the now familiar wall to follow it on its left side on an eastward course for the upper stretch of the Stonethwaite valley. The wall ends suddenly by the downfall of Pounsey Crag and thus cannot be rounded, therefore climbing it is unavoidable and demands careful attention. Beyond the wall a nasty little descent follows on steep bracken clad terrain for a straightforward crossing of Greenup Gill to join no less than the Cumbria Way path. Now you can wind down tired muscles on an enjoyable stroll back down this most picturesque of valleys. Continue on this path, passing the footbridge at the confluence of the gill and Langstrath Beck until the Stonethwaite bridge is reached. Cross this to reach the village, leaving nothing more than a short road walk back to the car, or a bit further on to the Borrowdale road for the service bus.

Route 5: Getting to Grips with Grasmoor & Co.

Walk File

Distance: 11¾ miles.

Total Ascent: 4300ft.

Start/Finish: Buttermere village.

Terrain: Clear paths following mostly grassy ridges. Rough ground on Whiteside.

Lakeland Maps: OS 1:25000 Outdoor Leisure series NW sheet no.4. Public Transport Bus service 77 Keswick – Buttermere. Mountain Goat Bus Keswick – Buttermere.

Features visited:

Whiteless Pike	2159ft
Wandope	2533ft
Grasmoor	2791ft
Hopegill Head	2525ft
Whiteside	2317ft
Rannerdale Knotts	1160ft

As far as most round trips go, this one is definitely something of a non-conformist. The OS map shows the Grasmoor group of fells linked together by a route taking the form of a rough 'M' shape rotated 90 degrees clockwise around its central point. In order to return to the original starting point, the two 'loose' ends have to be joined, and this can fortuitously be achieved by incorporating a very fine walk above the full length of the serene Crummock Water. The exciting little peak of Rannerdale Knotts cannot be ignored, and has been duly included; not as a 'sweeping up' operation, but because it is both a marvellous vantage point and a testing climb in its own right.

As you will already have noted, the high fells here are not situated around a natural line of directly connecting ridges, therefore a sizeable diversion needs to be made to the aforementioned Grasmoor, the highest

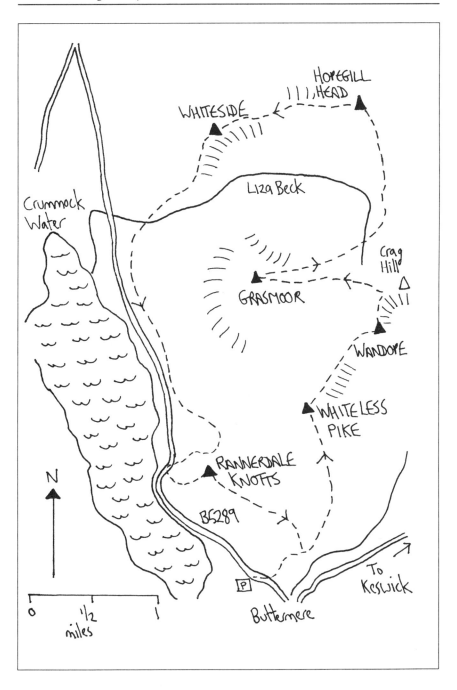

of the group, which would otherwise be left regrettably circumvented. To leave this near 2800ft mountain unclimbed would only serve to torture your conscience to the point where the only recourse would have to be a return visit at the earliest opportunity.

The starting point is Buttermere village, a handy base for numerous sorties into the high fells. A short way along the B5289 just before you reach the new National Trust car park on the left, a good path slants up immediately behind a couple of houses bound for Whiteless Pike. It soon leaves the intake wall, becoming a wide green track up to a large cairn at the crossroads of a number of paths. Continue on steepening ground along a meandering groove worn into the incline which facilitates the walking. The slope eases momentarily before a tiring climb to defeat the final 500ft slope, disappearing abruptly at the small flat top at 2159ft which is deserving of much more than the flattened heap of stones you will find there.

The wide view southward from this airy position is in total contrast to that directly ahead. Here you are confronted almost head on by the enormous bulk of Grasmoor which is well seen from such close quarters as is the route to your next goal, Wandope. One of Wandope's finest attributes is clear to see from Whiteless Pike, namely its tremendous rise in a sweep of a thousand feet from Third Gill.

A short descent on a series of rocky hummocks brings you to the small col at Saddle Gate, presenting an exacting approach with the eastern shoulder of Whiteless Edge falling away into the gorge below. Wandope's western spur which has the distinguished name of Thirdgill Head Man (although only indicated by a cairn on the 2½" OS map) is reached by keeping to the left branch of a split in the path, a neat top which is much better equipped to call itself highest point than is the summit proper.

A well beaten track can be easily picked out stretching away in the direction of Coledale Hause and avoiding the summit in the dash for Grasmoor. To ensure you do not miss out on Wandope's summit only a matter of yards away, take an eastward bearing to meet a very faint track leading directly to the tiny cairn at 2533ft. You will be glad you took the extra trouble to make this shortest of detours for this summit is a very fine situation. The cairn stands at the edge of the most impressive corrie of Addacomb Hole, with the southern flank of Crag Hill scarred by severe landslip occupying a major part of the view. From the summit, a narrow path appears in due course by persisting along the northwestern tract, but a much better option is to start off as though with the intention of climbing Crag Hill. A narrow well used path sticks to the very edge of the corrie but as the climbing starts you need to head back 'inland' northwestwards across the elevated grassy plateau.

Cross the Coledale track you previously ignored in favour of Wandope, to join up with the initially worn path blazing a trail up the easy east ridge of Grasmoor. If you think the ground here is eroded, console yourself with the fact that by following it you are able to avoid much worse on the straightforward direct descent to the Hause. After a short steepish pull the slope lessens into the summit expanse, with the main cairn and shelter still some distance further on. At 2791ft you have attained the 'big brother' of the Coledale massif with the gratifying prize of a panorama of a tremendous array of peaks.

From the summit another narrower track lying slightly north of your approach sticks to the rim of Dove Crags, but as the down-slope increases, can be difficult to trace in places. If weather conditions are against you, provided you maintain a northeastwards bearing, this will keep you sufficiently away from any difficulties and all you will have to negotiate is the grassy flank and some small rocky upthrusts further down the slope, to Coledale Hause via a simple crossing of Gasgale Gill.

From the Hause head north on grass at first, then up on a winding groove in the millions of rock fragments to gain the cairned subsidiary summit of Sand Hill, leaving an easy final stretch to Hopegill Head's very fine peaked top. Its most distinguished feature, the imposing Hobcarton Crag, plummets to the valley from directly beneath your feet, giving a real feeling of isolation and emptiness. The summit at 2525ft is the meeting place of three main ridges, Ladyside Pike to the north, Grisedale Pike to the east and that lying westward. Follow the latter ridge to your next destination, the highly under-rated Whiteside.

The next mile provides superb walking along the connecting ridge high above Gasgale Crags to the left which form a precipitous wall to the narrow valley of Gasgale Gill. After a small depression is reached on departing Hopegill Head, the path maintains an undulating ridge to the summit at 2317ft. Further along the edge, a cairn stands at a spectacular location only yards from a dramatic downward plunge. Grasmoor towers menacingly from across the steep valley, its sheer size obliterating a large part of the southern prospect.

The ridge begins to lose height as it extends further west, but still makes for a punishing descent on a very rough track. Some respite is gained on the final yards to Whin Ben, but immediately thereafter the slope resumes its relentless decline across a heathery flank to Liza Beck. The path swings round towards the Gasgale valley and meets a small wooden bridge which you should cross for the easy slopes just above the road at Lanthwaite Green. With Buttermere still some three miles away, a depressing route march on tarmac can thankfully be minimised by

Hopegill Head from Whiteside

taking a series of improving grass paths across Grasmoor's bracken clothed base.

The dessert which follows soon after digesting this most satisfying main course of mountains is provided by the diminutive Rannerdale Knotts, which soon comes into view up ahead. This is far from an insignificant hummock obstructing the throat of the Buttermere valley, as evidenced from this approach, with its northwest face with defending cross wall appearing near vertical; a mini version of Glencoe's Buachaille Etive Mor if ever there was.

As you near Rannerdale Farm the path draws away from the road and heads for High Rannerdale which divides the fell from Whiteless Pike. Cross the beck at a footbridge to follow the track on its opposite bank back around the base of Rannerdale Knotts, then through a gate and eventually emerging at a small car park by the roadside. A mere fifty paces on the Buttermere road brings you to a footpath/bridleway sign-post which indicates the day's last ascent.

The footpath route immediately strikes up a demanding gradient, grassy at first but getting increasingly rougher as the line of a short rock gully is joined. With Crummock Water seemingly beneath your feet, grass takes over again up to a small plateau which opens up previously unseen views to the north, with the narrowest of tracks to the right completing the final pitch to the first (and highest at 1160ft) of two prominent cairned tops. Separated by a distance of a matter of yards, it is well worth your while heading over to the other cairn which, sitting atop a rock plinth, requires some degree of dexterity to reach its highest stones.

Both tops are very much at the extremity of Rannerdale Knotts' tapering southeast ridge, which presents a leisurely and stress-free finale to the day. After a short rocky descent from the second cairn, the route continues along a wide grassy carpet in excellent condition, as though someone has dragged a giant lawnmower directly down the crest. At a slight rise this divides, with the left branch eventually arriving at the previously visited big cairn below Whiteless Pike. To get round having to cover the same ground twice, take the other equally good path directly down the easy slope through a muddy bit to a small gate to meet the road, to complete a detailed examination of this fine group of fells.

Route 6:
The Cream of Buttermere

Walk File

Distance: 12½ miles.

Total Ascent: 3600ft.

Start/Finish: Buttermere village.

Terrain: Good ridge paths involving a couple of steep descents. Some rough sections, notably the Haystacks approach.

Lakeland Maps: OS 1:25000 Outdoor Leisure series NW sheet no.4.

Public Transport: Bus service 77 Keswick – Buttermere. Mountain Goat Bus Keswick – Buttermere.

Features visited:

Red Pike	2479ft
High Stile	2644ft
High Crag	2443ft
Haystacks	1900ft
Fleetwith Pike	2126ft

Over the years, Buttermere has become a popular base for the high fells. A number of spectacular peaks more than satisfy the adventurous instincts of those who choose to visit their summits, and with comfortable accommodation including a fine youth hostel only a short walk from two excellent public houses, the days spent here are usually very full. If staying at the hostel, be warned that an arduous journey faces you back up the hill to your bed from the village watering holes after closing time.

This route crosses a marvellous ridge of high fells which are of almost equal height, rising steeply between the Buttermere and Ennerdale valleys, and commonly known as the High Stile Range after the highest of its peaks. The lower slopes on the Ennerdale side are cloaked with conifers, such is the considerable afforestation which has so changed the

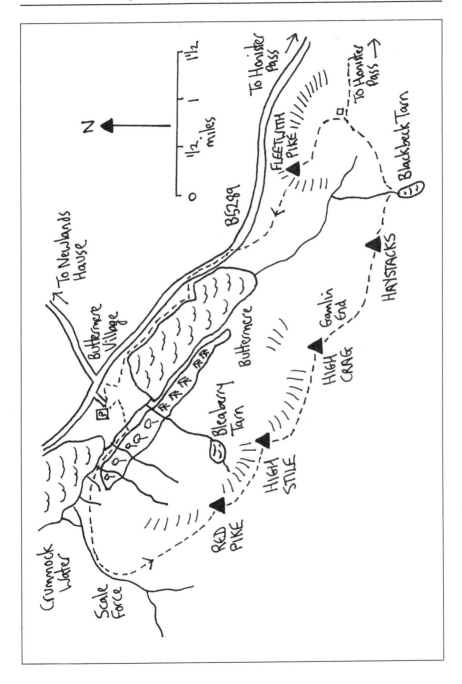

appearance of the valley. Today, few can recall Ennerdale before the arrival of the vast forest plantations.

Best for parking is by the Fish Hotel in the centre of Buttermere village, from where you are greeted by what appears to be an unassailable wall of rock split by the cascading waterfall of Sour Milk Gill. This area contains perhaps the best used route of access to the ridge, but today's offers an alternative in approaching the first of the day's fells, Red Pike, via the 'back door' and passing the magnificent Scale Force *en route*. From the Fish Hotel, follow a notoriously muddy lane away from the village. A gate on the right indicates the start of the 'short cut' lane to Scale Bridge and Scale Force.

High Crag from Buttermere

Cross the picturesque stone bridge to pick up the well trodden path heading right, alongside Buttermere Dubs in the direction of Crummock Water. In places the going can be very wet, so before setting out make doubly sure your boots have been adequately waterproofed.

The path never quite meets Crummock's lakeshore but gradually inclines away from it in traversing Red Pike's lower slopes. The route meets and for a short way follows the course of Scale Beck before revealing Scale Force itself, a tremendously powerful waterfall which is set in an imposing fissure. By scrambling over the rocks at its outflow, you can climb into the chasm itself where you can observe the sheer distance the water is having to plunge and feel its great intensity from very close quarters.

A steep track leaves the waterfall on its left side then, after climbing close by Scale Beck for a short distance, turns generally south-southeast-wards across a rocky and heathery slope to meet Lingcomb Edge, the true start of this exhilarating ridge. The final 700ft climb does not present any difficulties, and conveniently leads directly to Red Pike's summit at 2479ft. This compact top is an excellent viewpoint, situated at the edge of the ridge high above the twin corries of Ling Comb and Bleaberry Comb. Of the three major fells of the High Stile group, Red Pike has the distinction of being the only one having direct routes of ascent from both Buttermere and Ennerdale, the latter offering a way up via a small gap in the dense woodland.

The walk to High Stile is straightforward on a clear path by a line of iron posts, and in favourable weather conditions the fringe of the escarp-ment above Bleaberry Comb can be followed with confidence to the main cairn at 2644ft, another dramatic place for fine viewing. I would also strongly recommend a short detour along the rocky promontory to the northeast which divides Bleaberry and Burtness Combs. From here, any uncertainty you may have had as to why Red Pike is so named will be clarified, by way of the distinctively coloured soil of the now badly eroded path from Bleaberry Tarn.

Burtness Comb has no tarn, but is particularly well endowed with a most impressive set of crags. An easy undulating walk of little more than a mile around the rim of the comb leads to High Crag at 2443ft. From here the immense bulk of Pillar to the southwest makes compulsive viewing, with stiff competition provided by Great Gable and the Scafells, completing a mountain scene of the very highest quality.

Anyone who has toiled up the 1000ft scree ridden slope of Gamlin End cursing its unrelenting steepness will undoubtedly welcome the next half mile which descends it, skirting the knoll of Seat until level ground is reached at the Scarth Gap Pass, a well trodden route linking the But-termere and Ennerdale valleys. I consider myself to be personally jinxed here, as I cannot recall a time when I have descended Gamlin End in anything resembling settled weather. I also remember several years ago a friend of mine being blown over into me in gale force winds, cracking the arm of my glasses in the process. Fortunately they remained in one piece which avoided a myopia-enforced struggle on all fours.

From Scarth Gap, your next objective is Haystacks, the most curious of fells with its network of paths, craggy outcrops and picturesque summit tarns. There is quite simply nowhere else which compares with this unique place.

Continue on to pick up a decent path which thoughtfully winds its way through the roughest ground on its way to the highest point, marked by a pile of stones at 1900ft near to a tiny tarn. Haystacks may well be inferior in altitude to its neighbours, but has such a varied summit that to cover the whole area proves a fascinating exploration in itself.

Leave the summit along the clear path which passes close by Innominate Tarn (there have been calls to rename it after A. Wainwright as he made no secret of the fact that Haystacks was his great favourite), and the larger Blackbeck Tarn. A harsh winter will freeze solid the placid waters of the tarns, which calls to mind a photograph of me in tentative 'mountaineering' pose on the frozen surface of Innominate Tarn showing off my then new ice axe, taking great care for obvious reasons not to at that moment test out the sharpness of its point.

After proceeding northeast for a short way on a good track, the route splits, the left fork descending to the Buttermere valley. This path provides a valuable escape to safe ground, however the day's agenda shows that only one more summit is to be visited, Fleetwith Pike. If time is on your side ignore this change of direction and continue on the made path to cross the marshy little depression of Dubs Bottom. A brief re-ascent brings you onto the main Dubs Quarry track which has its beginnings at the top of the Honister Pass.

This track should be left almost straight away to join up with a faint grassy trod climbing by the left side of a distinctive climbing hut backed by a sizeable cairn. The path gets better with further climbing, eventually flanking Fleetwith's southern slope before swinging right to attain its big cairn at 2126ft. Fleetwith's major feature is sadly out of view from here in the shape of the tremendous buttress of Honister Crag, which falls away precipitously to the Honister Pass road and is a most imposing sight when travelling along it. Do not let this interfere with your enjoyment of what is a splendid all round view, particularly to the northwest in leading the eye along Buttermere, Crummock Water and even further onto Loweswater. It may seem totally remiss of me to mention this, but the surrounding high fells, well seen in their own right, always seem to take a back seat when presented with such an outstanding lake view.

With the Honister road appearing nothing more than a thin line traced on the wild valley landscape far below, a route of descent now forges ahead northwestwards down Fleetwith Edge. After an initial steep section of rocky clambering and scrambling, the gradient mercifully reduces into a grassy walk, but not for long as rock returns for the final drop down to Gatesgarth Farm. Just above the farm a waymarking arrow sends you off right in the direction of the Honister road to pick up an excellent zigzag path. Look out for Fanny Mercer's cross beneath a small crag to your left. The slope eventually peters out and meets the road a short walk from Gatesgarth, site of a Mountain Rescue Kit and setting for a recent series of 'One Man And His Dog'.

Relief from pounding the tarmac for the last two miles back to Buttermere can be had in that soon after the farm, where road meets lake the wooded lakeshore path can be joined. This is a most enjoyable finale, passing through a small rock tunnel along the way before returning to the village at Wilkinsyke farm to review the day's exploits over a well deserved beverage.

Route 7: Hitting The Heights above Ennerdale

Walk File

Distance: 14¾ miles.

Total Ascent: 4200ft.

Start/Finish: Forestry Commission car park, Ennerdale (GR. 086154 OS 2½" map, NW sheet).

Terrain: Grassy fells at first, becoming increasingly rougher eastward, and some interesting route finding in Ennerdale Forest. Good paths throughout.

Lakeland Maps: OS 1:25000 Outdoor Leisure series NW sheet no.4.

Public Transport: None.

Features visited:

Crag Fell	1716ft
Caw Fell	2288ft
Haycock	2618ft
Scoat Fell	2760ft
Steeple	2687ft
Pillar	2927ft

Despite the dense afforestation of its lower slopes, Ennerdale remains, and hopefully will always remain, a walker's retreat. With no motor road pushing through the valley floor, it has retained a certain mystique quite unlike anywhere else in Lakeland. Its high fells thrust defiantly above the tree line, as though out of reach beyond the tranquil Ennerdale Water. Elusive these fells may appear, but elusive they are not, and herein lies the challenge to the adventurer committed to a long day. The mass of high ground enclosing the valley to the south is dominated by the elegant lines of Pillar at the apex of this diverse round which encapsulates all that is best in Lakeland walking – the mountain ridge, the forest track and the lake shore path.

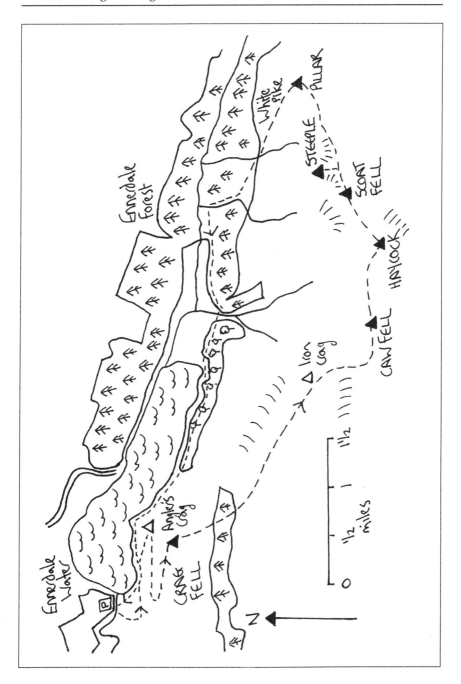

The best place for leaving the vehicle is the Forestry Commission car park near the western end of the lake. At the cottage beyond the car park entrance, head through the field on the right of Crag Farm House, turning left after crossing a stile to follow the woodland path immediately above the intake wall. This leads on to the main lake shore path, which you should keep to for a short distance before branching right along the thin track blazing a trail through the bracken in the direction of Anglers Crag. This significant headland creates a large kink in Ennerdale Water's southern shoreline, its appealing summit situated almost directly above it but easily attained by way of a minimal and strongly recommended detour. At only 811ft, the diminutive top is more a break in the steep northern flank of the aptly named Crag Fell than a summit in its own right, but nevertheless offers very fine views deep into the valley and towards what lies ahead.

To continue the climb, rejoin the Crag Fell track at a small connecting plateau, from where the route now slants beneath Revelin Crag. Once past this rock-face, the summit cairn at 1716ft is reached by turning immediately left past a couple of iron posts for a straightforward ascent on grass. Save for its near neighbour Grike (which incidentally makes an excellent short afternoon walk when coupled with Crag Fell), nothing obscures the fine westward aspect where land becomes sea.

A long and unfortunately rather tedious walk is now called for to join the main ridge at Caw Fell, which lies the best part of three and a half miles away to the southeast. Firstly, descend in this direction on a fair but periodically muddy track, where alongside you can indulge on the occasional bilberry if passing this way in late summer.

Stiles at either end allow a way into and out of the plantation which stands in the small hollow up ahead. Once through the trees you should now be able to distinguish the way ahead, in the form of a long grass track with a big wall on your left. Here is yet another of those amazing ridge walls, which remains with you for the next five miles all the way to Scoat Fell. This is a fact well worth bearing in mind if caught in a rapidly descending mist in this harsh terrain.

As if to break the monotony of the gentle grassy incline, the odd patch of rock pokes through, giving a subtle hint more exciting ground is now not too far away. After the traverse of Iron Crag, the wall switches its course to head east for Haycock and the 2500ft contour. Caw Fell boasts such an extensive top it is very tricky to make out its highest inches, although a walk to the cairn a quarter of a mile west from the aforementioned wall corner would at first glance seem to indicate the final yards to the summit. I will spare you this unnecessary extra distance as the fact is the true top at 2288ft actually lies in entirely the opposite direction, on the north side of the 'Haycock wall', above Silver Cove.

From Caw Fell, proceed with the wall as your guide, as the easy grass slopes enjoyed so far now begin to merge into much harsher terrain. The path gets forced off its usual course in passing around the sizeable rock tor of Little Gowder Crag, then swings back towards the wall in aiming for the summit cairn at 2618ft. A good shelter can be found on the Ennerdale side of the wall. Haycock is Lakeland's most westerly fell in excess of the 2500ft mark, and is also an excellent location for viewing the Scafells and the Scoat Fell/Steeple partnership which features next on the day's itinerary. I can also recall partaking of a plastic beaker of cheap wine (not full, I might add) in celebration of a friend's climbing of Haycock as his last of Lakeland's "big un's".

The rugged ground on Haycock's east side is short lived, with rock becoming less common in descending to a marked crossroads. The reascent of the grassy shoulder opposite is very gradual, ending with a leisurely stroll across Scoat Fell's level top. Although one of the region's biggest fells, this is not usually a place on which a lot of time is spent, for the simple reason that one of Lakeland hillwalking's very best short detours is made from here. I am referring to the magnificent pinnacle of Steeple, which stands a only matter of yards away to the north.

A small break in the summit wall reveals the biggest cairn, (but not representing its actual top as you will later discover) and a nearby shelter, from where the Steeple track begins. This takes an exciting course, in firstly descending to a small col, then heads left around a small outcrop before a short scramble to arrive suddenly at the peak itself, a rocky pulpit above Ennerdale's congregation of a million trees. One look over the edge into the depths of Mirk Cove will have your stomach somersaulting with sheer exhilaration, no matter how many times you do it.

The return journey to Scoat Fell by exactly the same route is by no means dull, as now its superb buttresses can best be appraised in regaining the ridge back at the plateau. In addition to being a valuable route indicator the now familiar wall is also home to the summit cairn. The small pile of stones curiously sits directly on top of it at its highest point, 2760ft. Methinks this is a cairn not often touched.

Almost as soon as the descent of Scoat Fell's eastern ridge begins the wall finally ends in a leftward bend, the rough track passing through it at a small gap. After a small patch of rocks and boulders, more level ground is reached for an easy walk across grass to a slight rise above Black Crag before a sharp descent to Wind Gap. The last 500ft to Pillar now rises above, and a number of routes, each one as rough as the next, can be followed up the shattered face. They ultimately converge into a well cairned path for the final yards to the summit shelter and OS column at 2927ft, a dominant view of the highest quality from one of the district's ten highest peaks.

As is the case with Helvellyn, Pillar too seems to have its own self-confident sheep, who have the uncanny ability to distinguish with ease the rustling of a crisp packet from a hundred yards in a driving head-wind. When one of them decides to clasp one end of your sandwich firmly in its teeth whilst ignoring the fact you are trying to frantically devour it from the other, it is better to accept defeat and thus avoid a sloppy ovine kiss, as a friend found recently.

Pillar from Steeple

Pillar is the end of the line as far as following the ridge goes, leaving you with a return journey across a wide variety of terrain to Ennerdale of some six and a half miles. A very well marked track, typical of Pillar's summit approaches, begins the descent along White Pike, the rocky northwest shoulder, rounding the entrance to a sheer gully on its left side, and lower down reaching a line of iron fence posts stretching down to a stile at the boundary of the tree line. Continue through the forest for a short way, then through a small section of cleared woodland to one of the many forest roads at a tiny bridge over the tumbling waters of High Beck.

Take this road until you reach a signpost, then turn right to drop down alongside a superb mossy ravine to cross a wooden footbridge. The narrow track immediately beyond brings you out on another forest road. After only fifty yards or so leave this on the right to meet up with a thin track which passes close by the silent and secluded pool of Moss Dub, before wending your way through the dense plantation to rejoin the road left a few minutes earlier. This is trodden for a near dead straight mile, then trends right for a crossing of a couple of stiles with Ennerdale Water at long last in your sights in the distance.

The lake shore path is nowadays trodden by huge numbers of long distance hikers as well as day walkers and ramblers, since A.Wainwright incorporated it into his Coast To Coast Walk in the early 1970s. The path now climbs very gently up to its roughest section in rounding the foot of Angler's Crag, after which returning to almost water level on to a stile at the lake's end. From here, only a short stroll remains past the pumping station and back to the car park, and maybe a detour to Ennerdale Bridge to join the 'Coast to Coasters' in the Fox and Hounds bar.

Route 8:
The Mountains of Mosedale

Walk File

Distance: 10½ miles.

Total Ascent: 4700ft.

Start/Finish: Car Park, Wasdale Head.

Terrain: Good paths and tracks the whole way, on very rough terrain. Some particularly steep ascents, descents and quite a bit of scrambling involved.

Lakeland Maps: OS 1:25000 Outdoor Leisure series NW sheet no.4 and SW sheet no. 6.

Public Transport: None.

Features visited:

Kirk Fell	2630ft
Pillar	2927ft
Scoat Fell	2760ft
Red Pike	2707ft
Yewbarrow	2058ft

Despite its remoteness and, much that I hate to mention, its reputation for slightly above average precipitation, the Wasdale valley draws many visitors, undoubtedly inspired by the mystique of Wastwater and the superb ring of peaks towering above the valley head. It is inevitable that sooner or later you too will find yourself travelling the narrow road hugging the lake shore in the knowledge that the hillwalker is spoilt for choice from any number of magnificent routes. As I have tasked myself with selecting one for this volume, the challenging round of the Mosedale valley is one of the finest and toughest to be had, a walk not to be missed.

Cars can be left in a large open field a short distance from the Wasdale Head Inn, which is well worth a look in (preferably after the day's adventures when the atmosphere can be savoured over refreshments) for its framed photographs of the pioneering rock climbers of a century

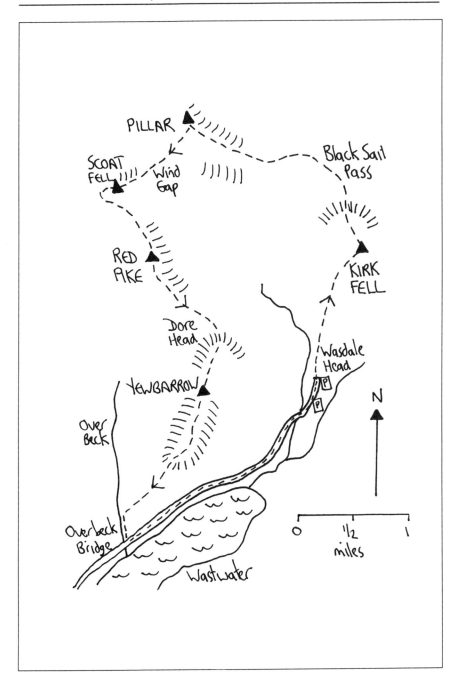

ago, who used the place as a base for their sorties into the then unexplored crags. Beyond the Inn is Row Head farm, whose grounds you should pass through to follow Mosedale Beck beyond the farm gate. Where the path swings left bound for the Black Sail Pass, continue straight ahead through a second gate for one of the rudest awakenings in Lake District hillwalking; the unrelenting ascent of Kirk Fell's south ridge.

This is a severe test of the calf muscles, initially on footsteps worn into the grassy slope, and with improving views left and right, sufficient motivation is provided to struggle on. With continued height gain the grass gives over to rougher terrain which on a gradient such as this does make life more difficult. It is a matter of keeping well right of the worst of the unstable rocks and stones to avoid dislodging anything which would no doubt be dispatched to the bottom of the hill in next to no time. After a couple of false dawns the steepness reduces leaving a straightforward trip following cairns to the 2630ft summit cairn and accompanying shelter. If there is anything positive to be said about this climb it must be that in just over a mile away is valley level at Wasdale Head, and now you are already surveying fellow 2500ft peaks from an excellent vantage point, making it all worthwhile.

Pillar is your next peak looming large beyond the Black Sail Pass, for which Kirk Fell must now be departed. A line of old fence posts and occasional cairns lead north-northwest as the path threads its way through Kirkfell Crags, necessitating a short rock scramble at a troublesome section. Progress becomes very tough in descending to the summit of the Black Sail Pass, before moving onto Pillar's tapering east ridge. The walking is easy at first across the grassy incline up to the fine viewpoint for upper Ennerdale where the path divides, the right branch forming the exhilarating traverse to Pillar Rock. Your route continues ahead, swinging left then right to take an intricate line through the many outcrops and boulders. In bearing left the cairned path then meets up with a line of old fence posts, and in some places very close to the edge of threatening craggy terrain.

Once the steep drops are past, an easy walk remains across to the OS column at 2927ft, summit cairn and shelter, a close knit community of fell-top artefacts atop the expansive plateau, and an excellent place to break off for lunch. A tremendous collection of peaks are displayed from Pillar, a real challenge of fell identification even to the most knowledgeable Lakeland afficionado.

A number of routes leave the summit, therefore if the mist is down, a quick check of the compass will set you off on the right course for Scoat Fell via Wind Gap, in heading west-southwest to meet a pronounced line of cairns leading on to a very loose scramble down to the col, an escape route for both Ennerdale and Wasdale. The climb immediately thereafter is rough, over a small boulder field, but once the top of Black Crag is reached, maintains a grassy level. A contouring offshoot path, which you should ignore, heads south bound for Red Pike and in doing so cuts off your intended objective, therefore continue west for another bouldery scramble above the bowl of Mirk Cove and on through a wall gap to emerge on Scoat Fell's spacious top. A small cairn stands on the wall itself, a most unusually sited highest point at 2760ft. With this as your guide, proceed along to the biggest cairn by a small rock shelter.

A nearby gap in the sturdy summit wall is the key for reaching Red Pike, which lies a mile to the southeast. After passing through it, you will soon discover the descending gradients of the connecting ridge are very gradual, making for gentle walking after all the roughness so far tackled. After the climbing recommences, this too quite straightforward, you will meet up with a fair track which forms a well used diversion from the contouring path, a favoured line in keeping to the left edge high above upper Mosedale and offering superb views of Pillar's crag-riddled southern face. The summit cairn at 2707ft sits along this track, spectacularly by the edge of the escarpment, but you may be surprised to learn Red Pike possesses another feature which captures more attention. Continue along the edge, whereupon paths merge leading on to a bigger cairn than that which crowns the summit but standing a few yards further on at a point some 80ft lower.

The Chair sadly remains un-named on the 2½" OS map, and maybe it is indirectly referred to as one of the 'Cairns' so mentioned. It is a collection of rocks cleverly fashioned into a large seat from where far reaching views can be had. You may even be required to wait your turn on a fine day before treating yourself to a few minutes on this high level throne.

This elaborate structure lies only slightly off the main route, easily rejoined by bearing left to a line of cairns heading south where a good track soon develops through rough terrain and which merges into another approaching from your left, the beginning of the link between Red Pike and the day's last top, Yewbarrow. The very distinct path presents no difficulty and makes for a long and pleasurable descent to Dore Head, the only disadvantage being the loss of some 1200ft of hard won height in the process.

Dore Head is well known for its huge scree shoot which provides a rapid descent into Mosedale for those hillwalkers in danger of missing last orders at the Wasdale Head Inn. There is perhaps another reason for its popularity, for one glance up at the previously innocent looking Yewbarrow from the col and you would be forgiven for concluding enough is enough for one day. Yewbarrow is however, a magnificent fell and here is an ideal opportunity to scale it.

There are two main routes, one easy, one not so easy. If you don't fancy the not so easy one, the summit can be gained by a traverse of the grassy incline slightly west of south from Dore Head. If you do, it is straight up the rocky flank of Stirrup Crag for you for more 'hands on'. A rough walk on a winding track very soon becomes a pulsating scramble with a little exposure, then once over the crag, on grass up to its cairn at the north end of the considerable summit ridge with the main top visible off in the distance.

Wastwater from Yewbarrow

A further twenty minutes tramping will bring you to the highest point at 2058ft, the end of the day's climbing. Despite the fact the summit ridge is long and flat, Yewbarrow is an isolated fell which rises quickly to the 2000ft contour from the valley floor. As such, routes of descent require the utmost concentration, particularly the one you will be following, along the southwest ridge to Overbeck Bridge. Shortly after departing the summit, an eroded path keeps to the thin undulating crest, revealing a marvellous sight of the whole length of Wastwater backed by its famous screes. The route skirts the top of Great Door, an awesome cleft in the rocky flank, before trending right to descend an extremely eroded gully between the buttresses of Bell Rib and Dropping Crag.

A good track avoids the very worst of the gully's loose stuff by switching sides from right to left part way down, to slant across the bracken clad base of the seemingly impenetrable crags, arriving at a stile crossing a large wall. A fence then takes over in accompanying a thin grass track down through bracken, the route then swinging left to a further gate, beyond which Over Beck is followed to a small secluded car park just off the road. Retrospective views of Yewbarrow from these latter stages of the descent are most impressive.

With fell territory now behind you, tarmac must be followed for just short of two miles for the return to Wasdale Head. If any road walk can be tolerated without complaint then I reckon this one must be top of the list, for having had the privilege of a day in the company of such fine fells, it is nigh on impossible to think negative thoughts.

Route 9: The Scafells (the Long Way)

Walk File

Distance: 15½ miles.

Total Ascent: 4800ft.

Start/Finish: Small car park by Wha House Farm, Eskdale.

Terrain: As rough as it gets in Lakeland, but magnificent with it. Navigational care essential in mist.

Lakeland Maps: OS 1:25000 Outdoor Leisure series SW sheet no. 6.

Public Transport: Ravenglass & Eskdale railway. BR station at Ravenglass.

Features visited:

Slight Side	2499ft
Scafell	3162ft
Scafell Pike	3210ft
Great End	2984ft
Esk Pike	2903ft

When long journeys are needed to get at a chosen route the determined hillwalker is rarely deterred. Eskdale is one of the more difficult of Lakeland's valleys to reach, and even before setting foot on the hills can prove quite a daunting prospect if approaching from the east in being confronted by the hairpin bends and steep gradients of the 1281ft Wrynose and 1291ft Hardknott passes, which appear rather innocuous on the 2½" OS map. The same cannot be said of them on the 1¼" Landranger map with its clusters of those infamous little black arrowheads covering the road, but be reassured in the fact that roads into the valley from the west are quite different, and I would recommend the fell road from Ulpha as a delightful alternative. The slim road through the valley passes close by the narrow gauge railway which runs through to the coast at Ravenglass some seven miles away. Its Eskdale terminus falls

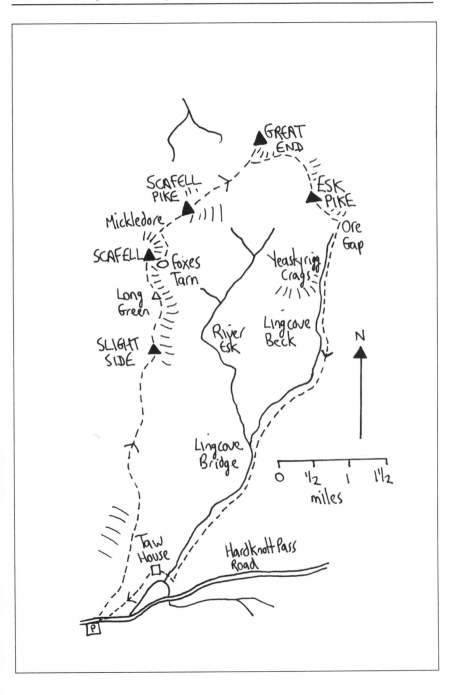

only a couple of miles short of this route into Lakeland's highest fells, encircling the upper reaches of a wild and beautiful valley.

What will be a long day begins from the small parking area by the roadside opposite the entrance to Wha House farm. A nearby stile gives access to the open fell-side. The complex terrain immediately in view contains no direct route and as a result the path steers clear of it, instead choosing to slant across the lower slopes just above the intake wall, passing through a big sheepfold *en route*.

A good deal of bracken is encountered as wall and path part company, the latter keeping well right of a small area of marsh. The day's first top, Slight Side, soon comes into view looking much further away than it actually is, but after a small rise the full extent of its slopes can be seen across a second, and much larger plateau. The prominent ridge to your left may at first appear to be the next landmark to reach, but it is ignored in favour of the direct approach through the upland level and its many boggy bits. You will no doubt have noticed the numerous cairns so far, and one even sits atop an enormous rock beneath the route's first gradient of any note. The now roughened track forges through scree then rock, and as the ground flattens out, skirts right of Slight Side's summit. A couple of small cairns stand a few yards apart balanced on the highest rocks at 2499ft, a superb viewing station for the miles so far covered and also the peaks of the Scafell massif now tantalisingly well within reach.

Having returned to the main path, Scafell itself looms very large up ahead. The route keeps excitingly close to steep drops into upper Eskdale and becomes increasingly rougher underfoot once the cairned top of Long Green is reached, towering over the popular Cam Spout path climbing to Mickledore. A further short climb opens up Scafell's vast stony top, across which a clear track runs to facilitate the last few yards to the summit cairn at 3162ft, once thought to be England's highest ground until resurveying relegated it to second place.

Scafell is a superlative viewpoint, not least for the dramatic close ups of its awesome crags and precipices which comprise some of the most challenging climbing rock in the country. Indeed the early pioneers of the sport practised their technique on these very rock-faces at the turn of the century, and considering the quality of the equipment then at their disposal, their achievements were all the more remarkable.

With England's second highest mountain beneath your feet, all you could possibly settle for next is the biggest of the lot, Scafell Pike, clearly in view to the northeast. Although less than a hundred feet separate the two in terms of altitude, close on a thousand feet of climbing is necessary to the Pike.

Foxes Tarn, Scafell.

All routes off the hill in this direction are excellent. Lord's Rake and the West Wall Traverse in Deep Gill are narrow and enclosed with loose rock and thus can be awkward if you meet anyone coming up, a highly likely scenario as both are well used to the point of being overwalked. Broad Stand is the most direct, but is more for serious scramblers and climbers, which leaves what I find the least stressful way off, via Foxes Tarn.

With a purposeful stride, follow the superbly constructed stairway of inlaid rocks down the rough east flank to the celebrated 'puddle' of Foxes Tarn, with only just enough grass nearby to accommodate perhaps a couple of tents; the wildest of wild camps. Follow the line of the tarn's issuing stream into a thin gully of loose rock and scree to meet up with a track parallel to the Cam Spout track to finally commence the climb to Scafell Pike. The first 200ft or so will bring you up to the 'pass' of Mickledore, a vital escape route for Eskdale and Wasdale Head from this potentially hazardous mountain terrain.

My first visit to the Scafells was rather fortuitous to say the least. One overcast Spring Sunday morning equipped with sufficient maps to cover the whole of Lakeland, with no firm plans two of us had succeeded in hitching a lift from Kendal. We very much liked the idea of the Cam Spout route into the Scafells therefore we optimistically ventured Eskdale as our destination to the driver, but would have settled for somewhere much nearer. To our amazement, he happily agreed to take us wherever we wished, as he was simply out for a tour of the countryside. An hour and two mountain passes later we found ourselves in Eskdale and Cam Spout bound, speechless at our good luck.

From the pass, cairns every few yards navigate a good line through the vast boulder field up to Scafell Pike. This abundance of raw material has been put to good use, for close by and dwarfing the OS column stands an immense cairn complete with steps, an elevated platform from which to appreciate a spectacular all round view. I have seen its height quoted as both 3206ft and 3210ft. If you hog the cairn for too long you will start to get disapproving looks from new arrivals wanting their turn, so with a smug expression of satisfaction, step down and search out a place for a long deserved lunch interval.

The summit area is littered with shelters of varying degrees of construction, and through these the path threads its way to the respective cols of Broad Crag and Ill Crag. Yet more cairns mark the way across yet more boulders, where in bad weather a cool head will avoid going astray. Soon after the last of the concentration of boulders, the going becomes less arduous with Great End up ahead. Leave the main path bound for Esk Hause for the short ascent to its summit, only yards from a plunge of immense crags.

We have seen some British mountains being elevated to the higher echelons by the building of outsized cairns. That which once crowned the 3984ft Ben Lawers in Scotland's Southern Highlands was constructed to make up a sixteen-foot deficiency to attain the elusive 4000ft contour, but did not survive the elements. Maybe someone will one day emulate the feat on the 2984ft Great End to give it English 'Munro' status.

The Great End offshoot path now needs to be rewalked to again join the way down to Esk Hause. Just above its famous cross wall shelter, follow the clear track branching southward in the direction of Esk Pike. A direct climb of the rocky defences of its northwest slope is avoided by the path diverting right.

At a cairn positioned on a flat slab, the path turns left through less difficult ground, aiming for the summit cairn. A small pile of stones atop a solid rock base indicates the highest point at 2903ft, a tremendous location for a considerable number of high fells, not least the route followed thus far.

Continue on southeast then east from the summit for the short descent to the rust-coloured ground of Ore Gap. The depression is usually a halting place on the way to Bowfell, but today it marks your turning point for the very long return through the full length of upper Eskdale. It is surprising to find nothing more than a thin strip of flattened grass representing the route leaving the Gap, however a clearer track does eventually form further down the slope. By bearing left of the very boggy ground flanking Yeastyrigg Gill you will join the better path coming down from Three Tarns. The gill flows into Lingcove Beck, whose left bank should be maintained for an excellent appraisal of Esk Pike, appearing as a commanding peak from this angle. The good path then swings round above a series of picturesque waterfalls down to pass Lingcove Bridge, a distinctive landmark of the valley.

By the bridge Lingcove Beck merges into the River Esk. The path continues through fields with the river close by, crossing it at a sturdy footbridge for Taw House. The way to the farm is well and truly enclosed to avoid trespass, squeezed between wall and fence with stiles at each end. Pick up the farm track to the surfaced road for the short walk back to the car park, with the muck of England's highest peaks on your boots as a souvenir of a memorable day.

Route 10:
From Ulpha to The Sea

Walk File

Distance: 15 miles.

Total Ascent: 3600ft.

Start: Ulpha, Duddon Valley.

Finish: Silecroft.

Terrain: Featureless moorland. Very few clear paths, several marshy areas.

Lakeland Maps: OS 1:25000 Outdoor Leisure series SW sheet no. 6 (as far as Buckbarrow). OS 1:50000 Landranger series Sheet no 96 Barrow-In-Furness.

Public Transport: None to Ulpha. BR station at Silecroft (West Coast line).

Features visited:

Hesk Fell	1566ft
Yoadcastle	1610ft
Stainton Pike	1632ft
Whit Fell	1876ft
Buckbarrow	1799ft
Stoneside Hill	1383ft
Black Combe	1970ft

Tucked away in the far southwest corner of the Lake District National Park is a procession of rounded hills which the forces of nature have arranged into a long ridge displaying little deviation from due north. With the exception of Black Combe at its end, the ridge shows little evidence of hillwalker popularity, and despite the fact the 2000ft contour is only threatened and never actually breached, some considerable effort is still called for to link together a total of seven summits in ultimate quest of the West Cumbrian coastline.

The small village of Ulpha in the Duddon Valley is your starting point,

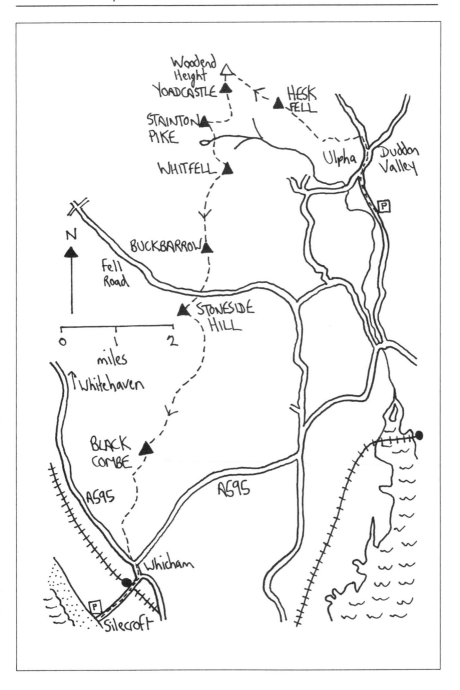

which cannot be reached through public transport. If your choice is to make use of two cars, Ulpha itself is not good for parking, therefore the best place to leave one of them is in an old quarry a mile away on the Broughton-in-Furness road, marked on the 2½" OS map. This does of course mean an extra mile's walk back to the village, avoidable by bribing a friendly chauffeur to drop you off and pick you up at the seaside.

Follow the Eskdale road climbing very steeply through woodland out of Ulpha. Once out of the trees, the road levels and a signpost at a gate can be seen up on the left. This indicates a public footpath which has actually become rather overgrown, marshily crossing the first field to a wall gap, in the direction of Baskill farm. Once through the gap, aim for the gate at the right edge of the buildings, and immediately on through another to gain access to a path between walls. With the succinctly named 'Pike' up ahead, take the rightmost gate to slant up through a large field to pick up a thin track leading to a further gate in its top corner.

Finally you are out in open country bound for Hesk Fell. The good path which begins to ascend its southeast flank soon gives up the ghost in favour of contouring left, leaving you to make your own way up the grassy expanse to the collection of a half dozen stones at its highest point of 1566ft. Featureless the top may be, but as a vantage point it is beyond criticism, with many of the high peaks of Lakeland's southwestern sector well seen from a refreshing new angle.

Hesk Fell stands aloof from its neighbours, therefore an unavoidable depression must now be crossed. As you have set yourself up for a complete traverse of the main ridge, aim in the direction of its rightmost top, Woodend Height. Due to the fact no defined route exists, my only advice is to look out for the wettest bits whilst minimising your height loss. Once the climbing begins again, a very faint grassy trod can be picked up heading for Woodend's parent fell, Yoadcastle. This track soon splits, with the right arm bending round to the northern extremity of the ridge. The shapely cairn on Woodend Height overlooks the isolated Devoke Water, and for those 'in the know', its surrounding hills make a remote short walk.

Your next summit is Yoadcastle itself, and a good one it is, involving no more than a ten minute trip finishing with a clamber up its rocky ramparts to the highest point at 1610ft, with fine open views of the coastal sweep which always seem dominated by Sellafield's vast complex. Back inland, the view-obliterating bulk of Whit Fell tends to dominate the immediate scene rather more than the fell standing slightly right of the natural line of the ridge, Stainton Pike. The route to it begins far from directly, heading east at first to round a grassy mound, then turning sharp right below a small outcrop to a wire fence, which you must cross to gain its big cairn at 1632ft.

Devoke Water from Woodend Height.

In heading directly for the grassy slopes of Whit Fell you will eventually return to straddle again the aforementioned fence at a waterlogged depression containing Holehouse Tarn. For the first time in the day, traces of a distinct path begin to emerge. Follow its right fork when it splits at the foot of the slope, and for a quick and direct assault on the summit, do the same again at a further division. The greatest altitude reached thus far, measuring 1876ft, is a curious place. Near to an OS column, welcome evidence you are not the second person (after myself) in the history of mankind to have climbed the hill, stands a considerably larger cairn on a pile of stones with an accompanying shelter. With Whit Fell beneath your feet comes the best southward view you have been able to appreciate all day.

To avoid a substantial loss of height into the remote valley of Sele Bottom which lies due south, by bearing southwest from Whit Fell you will pick up a thin track, passing by an isolated pile of stones which someone has fashioned into a useful waymarking cairn. The dome of Burn Moor is then traversed before dropping down through some very unpleasant and sadly unavoidable bog. The territory immediately beyond is much better, and offers an intricate scramble through rocks to the equally rocky top of Buckbarrow at 1799ft. Before your spirits sink at the sight of Black Combe looking enormous and miles away, I would like to take this opportunity to reassure you this is a trick of the eye on both counts, so you can take a well earned break amongst Buckbarrow's outcrops and look forward to what lies ahead with renewed vigour.

As Buckbarrow's summit is defended by rough terrain, its southern rocks must be negotiated to meet up with the grassy track beyond. This keeps close to the line of a wall and descends very gently to the Corney Fell road on the 1300ft contour. The continuation of the Buckbarrow wall marks the way up the short slope to the small peak of Stoneside Hill at 1383ft, well detached from the Black Combe massif but sufficiently elevated to be a useful place from which to seek out a good line to the day's main summit.

As the wall turns to the left so does the track, descending through bracken to a large sheepfold by a small plantation. One hot summer afternoon, not having said a word to anyone for some five hours since being turfed out of the car at Ulpha, I met a gentleman by this plantation and we struck up a conversation concerning our respective achievements of the day. He got out his map to show me his route thus far, of a type and with colours I had previously not come across. It transpired the map was of cloth coated design which he had bought with his pocket money in the late 1940s when a lad. I suggested to him it might be worth something as it was in extremely good condition. If it could look like that after nearly fifty years of use, then there was probably little point consigning it to the bottom drawer in favour of a more modern version; this was a model built to last.

A long, dreary and pathless climb across the bleak Swinside Fell now awaits, calling for a summoning of mental and physical resolve in order to successfully navigate the tussocky grass, bogs and occasional fences. Once the slope eventually eases, the impressive Black Combe Screes are revealed, with the fell-top getting closer with every step.

The day's best path so far is still really no more than yet another slim track, but this time making navigation easy through being clearly visible stretching away up the gently rising northern flank. After all that has been encountered, the sheep-trimmed summit dome offers welcome relief as the highest point comes into view. The weather beaten OS column at 1970ft is protected by a circular stone shelter, but unfortunately the vast summit plateau of the day's final fell diminishes its overall quality as a viewpoint. Nevertheless, it does make a pleasant change to stand atop 'that big isolated hill to the south' which features in so many Lakeland perspectives.

Black Combe has little in common with its neighbours. Here is a hill which is climbed a lot, and mostly from the hamlet of Whicham, your next destination. By continuing southwest across the plateau you will meet the main path, wide, worn and stony in its early stages, and with magnificent open sea views. The route of descent takes a gradual contouring line through heathery slopes, becoming a grassy strip amongst dense bracken lower down, terminating at a gate and stile. Turn left onto a vehicle track above the intake wall which merges into a narrow surfaced lane. A short cut next to St. Mary's church brings you out at a small car park just off the main A595.

A mile's road walking into Silecroft village and on to its excellent beach (where hopefully your carriage awaits) completes the day, for a deserved foot soak in the icy Irish Sea.

Route 11:
Connecting Coniston's Peaks

Walk File

Distance: 14¼ miles.

Total Ascent: 4300ft.

Start/Finish: Coniston.

Terrain: Rough and exposed mountain walking on distinct paths and tracks throughout.

Lakeland Maps: OS 1:25000 Outdoor Leisure series SW sheet no. 6.

Public Transport: Bus service 505 & 506 Ambleside – Coniston.

Features visited:

Walna Scar	2037ft
Dow Crag	2555ft
Coniston Old Man	2631ft
Brim Fell	2611ft
Grey Friar	2536ft
Great Carrs	2575ft
Swirl How	2630ft
Wetherlam	2502ft

A first sighting from the A591 between Windermere and Ambleside of Wetherlam rising proudly from across the lake gives an indication that the isolated land-mass of the Coniston Fells should not be so dominated by its much publicised Old Man. Indeed, Wetherlam and Coniston Old Man stand at each end of an extremely popular ridge walk from Coniston, in itself a fine route, but with the disadvantage of leaving out a number of the group in the process. This route offers a solution to 'bring the family together' by way of a demanding expedition in taking in all the peripheral tops around the main ridge of the group.

From the town centre, follow the road signposted for the Sun Hotel

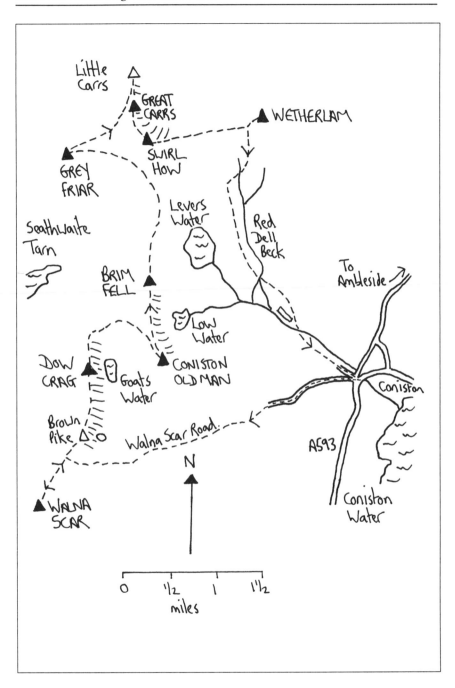

Inn. Just after the Inn, bear left then sharply right for the Walna Scar 'road', passing the site of the old railway station to the left. The slender surfaced road climbs straight away, providing a real kick start to the system. The first mile or so is simply a matter of pounding the tarmac until a gate is reached which signifies the beginning of fell territory proper. Many hillwalkers take advantage of the open spaces to be found immediately beyond the gate to leave the vehicle and thus cut out the road section on foot, but such a course of action is not really convenient for this route, so be reassured your efforts to date have not been in vain.

With Walna Scar fell up ahead, proceed along the infinitely more accommodating bridle way which is pushed ever so gradually away from the fells by the craggy flank of Coniston Old Man. A short way after the main track splits into two, the right branch offering a route of ascent to the Old Man itself, you will come upon Boo Tarn. Here is a reed festooned sheet of water, and one of the smallest ever to have acquired 'tarn status', and was of no concern whatsoever to a solitary mallard who, as I recently observed, was thoroughly enjoying himself splashing around in the sun drenched waters.

After rounding the Old Man's lower slopes, more of the high level traverse comes into view in the form of Brown Pike. The track next meets the youthful Torver Beck at Cove Bridge, somewhat spoiled in appearance by the addition of handrails, but nevertheless an excellent place for viewing the impressive hanging valley backed by the plunging slopes of Dow Crag.

The track becomes more rocky as it climbs to its summit cairn at Walna Scar Pass at almost 2000ft, continuing over into the Duddon Valley. Only a short simple climb to the left is needed to reach the first summit of the day. Although an outlier of the group at 2037ft, Walna Scar fell should be regarded as worthy of inclusion, therefore I have done just that.

Having ambled back down to the top of the pass, the way ahead is clear. A worn path starts up the grassy flank opposite, becoming rougher on the approach to the stone strewn summit of Brown Pike. With Blind Tarn sitting below, the path now takes to the edge of a spectacular escarpment *en route* for its greatest elevation at Dow Crag. Buck Pike is first crossed as the path maintains the crest, passing the outlets of several tremendous gashes in the vertical rock-face. A superb summit at 2555ft is attained by way of a short scramble over the topmost rocks, revealing the shimmering Goats Water a frightening thousand feet directly below your feet. There is no getting away from the fact that the eye of the hillwalker will more often than not be drawn towards the highest ground, but I would ask you make an exception here to view the resplendent Harter Fell. Now you are free to admire the Scafells.

A number of cairns show the way off Dow Crag to Goats Hause. From the depression you have a choice of paths to Coniston Old Man, one wide, one narrow. Both are a quick way up to the summit at the southernmost extremity of the major high level backbone of the Coniston group. With every upward pace the awesome scale of Dow Crag's rock wall complete with climbers is brought into view. At 2631ft there is no higher point reached than the Old Man, albeit by only twelve inches. Here is a place which lodges in the memory for two main reasons; firstly its unusual summit indicator of a massive slate plinth and large cairn and secondly for being one of the most populous irrespective of climatic conditions due to the emergence over the years of a 'tourist route' from Coniston. In its own right this is a fine climb with the bowl of cliffs towering over Low Water the highlight, but erosion has become very serious here and this side of the fell needs a chance to recover.

Brim Fell and Dow Crag.

Double back to pick up the unmistakeable path heading north. To refer to the stroll to 2611ft Brim Fell as a climb is really overstating things, as all of 50ft of height is gained on departing the Old Man. If it wasn't for its massive shaped cairn, and for the fact the OS map shows a couple of contour lines encircling it, you would most likely press on unaware that you'd traversed a rise on the ridge. The descent to Levers Hause presents no difficulty, but you should keep an eye out for a small cluster of boulders part way up the climb opposite. These are an important marker for the narrow trod which splits away from the main path to the left. By following this unfrequented route which proves intermittent in places, you can treat yourself to an excellent mile observing Seathwaite Tarn and the Tarn Beck valley whilst reeling in Grey Friar.

Lying as far to the west of the main ridge as it does, Grey Friar is more a part of the scenery of Wrynose and Duddon, as evidenced by its main lines of ascent. From the small cairn at the crossroads of Fairfield col, a short climb will bring you to its cairn at 2536ft, an outstanding point for the main ridge and the prominent peaked Dow Crag.

Back at the col, an interesting option to making a bee-line to Great Carrs is to pick up the narrow track snaking away northeastwards. This clever little track ensures a visit to yet another outlier, Little Carrs. From this subsidiary top most descend rapidly by Wet Side Edge to the top of the Wrynose Pass, but for you the long return to Coniston starts here. Head south on the rough path which blazes a trail to Great Carrs at 2575ft. The cairn commands a wide view, located at the very edge of a plunging cliff, from where Swirl How stands out across the chasm.

The track rounds the top of Broad Slack, appropriately named 'Top of Broad Slack' on the OS map. A few yards down the grassy flank in the direction of Grey Friar lies a small part of the wreckage of a plane which crashed into its upper slopes. A small wooden cross with a plaque inscribed 'Halifax Bomber – Oct 22nd 1944', makes a simple memorial to a tragic accident. Switching due east, the route now makes for Swirl How on a wide path up to the elegant cairn at 2630ft, the high point of several significant short ridge walks from near neighbours. The complete scene features many high fells, lakes, and tarns.

An interesting ridge now follows along the curiously named Prison Band. Sadly you will find yourself sentenced to only a half hour term of walking here as the Band is only short, however its angled ridge of rocky outcrops is sufficiently narrow and exposed to add spice to the descent to the massive cairn at Swirl Hause.

Several years ago I remember walking the main Coniston ridge, but then deliberately descending from this particular Hause bound for Levers Water. I was with someone who was then relatively new to the delights of the hills, but quite unlike myself, was a devoted fisherman keen to pluck something from its icy waters. Sections of fishing rod and various bits of tackle therefore had to accompany the usual contents of the rucksack that day, probably resembling some sort of radio backpack complete with 'antenna' bending in all directions under the strain of the gusting winds. These winds were equally as strong by the reservoir, resulting in the baited line repeatedly coming back in our faces almost as quickly as it had been cast. Few succeeded in hitting the water and needless to say we had to give up without success. Lucky it was fish for tea when I arrived home.

From Swirl Hause with all but one of the day's distinct tops surmounted, the last is now within easy reach in the shape of Wetherlam. The path starts up the slope, meeting a lengthy and undulating summit ridge. With fine northward views, and keeping well left of the secondary top of Black Sails, the main cairn at 2502ft soon comes underfoot.

Leave Wetherlam's top by your route of approach, but instead of retracing steps all the way back to Swirl Hause, look out for a narrow grassy trod branching off left just before a large cairn. This route eventually crosses the upper reach of Red Dell Beck, then proceeds to follow it down via an intermittent track, passing by a number of old shafts. The beck is recrossed at a small footbridge to join a level green path beyond a ruinous mine building. This excellent path contours the steep flank above Coppermines Valley, gaining level ground by a row of cottages.

Follow the wide road down until it can be left by crossing the Miners Bridge at the point where Church Beck takes over from the confluence of Levers Water and Red Dell becks. The way back to Coniston now follows the early stages of the 'tourist' route to Coniston Old Man, a gentle finish to round off a magnificent day.

Route 12:
Linking Langdale Ridges

Walk File

Distance: 14¾ miles.

Total Ascent: 5850ft.

Start/Finish: New Dungeon Ghyll Hotel, Great Langdale

Terrain: Tough walking over some of Lakeland's roughest ground, but following a number of the best known paths. Includes an exposed scramble (Jack's Rake).

Lakeland Maps: OS 1:25000 Outdoor Leisure series SW sheet no. 6.

Public Transport: Bus service 516 Ambleside – Dungeon Ghyll.

Features visited:

Pavey Ark	2288ft
Harrison Stickle	2415ft
Loft Crag	2270ft
Pike O'Stickle	2323ft
Rossett Pike	2106ft
Bowfell	2960ft
Crinkle Crags	2816ft
Cold Pike	2259ft
Pike O'Blisco	2304ft

For picking off a batch of renowned summits with consummate ease there is nowhere better than Lakeland's Langdale Pikes. This close knit quartet are tremendously popular and a fine Bank Holiday weekend sees them suffering under intense hillwalker pressure, for as a circuit in its own right the traverse of the group measures a compact five miles. To satisfy a greater thirst the Pikes are here included as part of a round high above the head of Great Langdale. Although not over long in mileage terms much rugged terrain is encountered, which when combined with

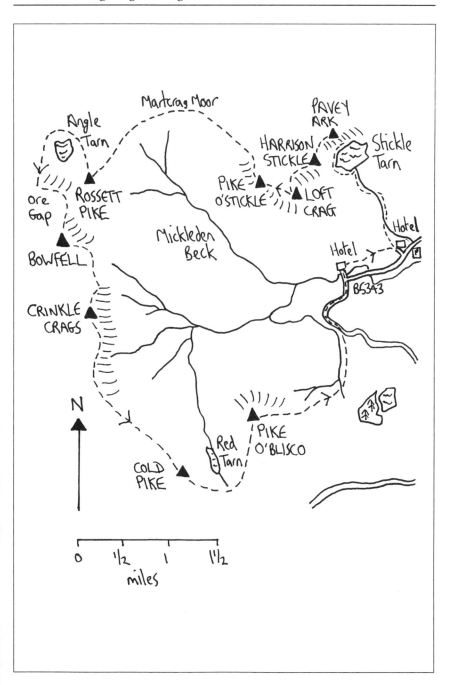

the total ascent covered of almost twice the three thousand feet of a typical high level route, makes a splendid day long traverse.

Begin from the car park opposite the lane to the New Dungeon Ghyll Hotel. Pass the hotel and Stickle Cottage into open country to join the heavily repaired path alongside Stickle Ghyll. Very little now remains of this first mile which hasn't had to be reconstructed. Cross the bridge to follow the ghyll on its right bank for an increasingly bouldery climb. Where the path disappears at a small rock wall, a number of large rocks ease a second crossing of the ghyll for the short ascent to the peaceful surroundings of Stickle Tarn. Paradoxically the tarn once provided the main water supply for the now defunct Elterwater gunpowder works.

Pavey Ark is your first target, and from tarn level it is difficult to concentrate on anything other than its forbidding cliff. A number of routes to the peak can be had, with the best and most challenging without doubt taking advantage of the natural break in the defences of the massive rock wall. Round the western shore of the tarn to climb the short scree slope at its base to begin the ascent of the angled rock shelf of Jack's Rake.

The Rake is definitely not for those of a nervous disposition. For a large part of the way up the shelf can be likened to a shallow cutting in the rock which reduces the exposure on its left side, but giving nowhere near the feeling of security as provided by the rock walls which enclose Lord's Rake on Scafell. There are a couple of awkward little sections, and recently I suffered a sad and unsettling experience in coming upon a sheep lying dead on the narrow path which judging by its appearance, had probably only just fallen from the top of the crag.

Towards the end of the traverse the path switches back towards the airy top at 2288ft. Western approaches pale into insignificance by comparison, confirmed by the view across the benign slopes of Thunacar Knott and High Raise which together make up a featureless foreground.

Intermittent cairns line a generally muddy track which leaves the summit to the southwest for a half mile's walk contouring above the Stickle Tarn basin to Harrison Stickle's cairn at 2415ft. Its position towards the southern extremity of the group of fells which occupy Lakeland's centre make Harrison Stickle a prominent subject of many views. A small area of boggy level ground lies between the three main summits of the Langdale Pikes, which can cause confusion in mist, which reminds me of one particular foul weather occasion bumping into someone on the summit of Harrison Stickle who had spent the previous half hour walking full circle in an unsuccessful attempt to reach Pike O'Stickle.

Pick up the main path heading west in the direction of Pike O'Stickle, but leave it after the second set of stepping stones in the marshy depression to detour left for Loft Crag at 2270ft. This is yet another of the day's exceptional vantage points, another rocky top which vies with its higher neighbours for the best aerial view of the valley. The path to the last of the Pikes hugs the edge of the ridge before dropping down to the head of a massive scree run now closed off to walkers.

The south scree as it is known, is a place of considerable historical importance, for in 1947 one of the main sites of the manufacture of stone axes was discovered there. Large numbers of poor quality implements were strewn on the slopes, considered unsuitable for use by those who fashioned them thousands of years ago. It is believed Neolithic man put the fruits of his labours to use in the clearing of forest land to create small settlements and grow crops. Sites have now been identified on each of the three Langdale Pikes. From the head of the scree, you have no alternative but to scramble up the buttress on a narrow winding track to attain the finest summit of the Langdale Pikes at 2323ft above slopes which fall away dramatically to Mickleden far below.

The next section to Rossett Pike may on the face of it appear the least demanding, but appearances can be deceptive. Head northwest on a fair track which crosses Martcrag Moor *en route* for the Stake Pass. A short distance after the cluster of tarns the path bisects, contour around to the west to join the path descending into Mickleden. At the point the path crosses Stake Gill, look out for a few cairns marking a very indistinct track rising up the slope to the right. A prolonged climb follows along Rossett Pike's eastern shoulder to the cairn at 2106ft. Its dimensions would usually ensure Rossett Pike acclaim as an outstanding peak, but not here as it is rarely given a second glance by those emerging from Rossett Gill aiming determinedly for bigger and better things.

The Langdale – Esk Hause 'motorway' is nearly always populated by walkers striding out for the Scafells, but you need not follow it any further than Angle Tarn *en route* for Ore Gap. A draining climb follows on a good path which strikes up the fell-side just beyond the tarn to the marked depression between Esk Pike and your next milestone, the majestic Bowfell. The cairned path winds its way through a sea of stones to its rocky crown at 2960ft, a summit which demands at least a half hour rest, to appreciate the multitude of peaks which make up this superlative viewpoint.

Leave the summit to the southeast to join the main ridge path which skirts the top of the Great Slab, a remarkable geological feature. A very worn cairned path makes light of the gradient on its descent to the busy col of Three Tarns, whose name leaves absolutely nothing to the imagination. From the tarns, the path meanders with aplomb amongst difficult and diverse terrain in surmounting the five prominent outcrops which comprise the rocky ridge of Crinkle Crags, which rises to its greatest height, 2816ft, at crinkle number two. The first major spur the route crosses from the Three Tarns approach is Shelter Crags, which is set slightly apart from the Crinkles themselves but nevertheless is occasionally mistaken for one of the five.

From the highest crinkle the last of the group now lies across an innocent looking little depression, but the main path leaving the highest point disappears abruptly at what has become known as the 'Bad Step'. It looks very awkward, but good holds on the ten foot pitch facilitate the scrambling. A much easier route circumvents the step on its west side, a fact I shamefully withheld from my wife on her first traverse of the ridge

The Bad Step, Crinkle Crags.

as I did not wish to alarm her. To her credit she did not back out, although I seem to recall few pleasantries were exchanged for the remainder of that particular journey.

After the steep descent from the final crinkle the walking becomes infinitely easier on a wide path which sees plenty of use, being a major route for the Crinkles and Bowfell from the high level start at the summit of the Wrynose Pass. Cold Pike's 2259ft summit stands a stone's throw from the main thoroughfare, and is worth the short detour.

Next is Red Tarn which lies beneath the southwest flank of the ninth and final peak of the day, Pike O'Blisco. A good track blazes a trail up the steep incline to reveal a view from the small top which provides more than ample reward for your efforts. A much smaller pile of stones than the shapely cairn which once stood at the highest of two tops now indicates the summit at 2304ft, towering over the Langdale valley.

The northeastern slopes fall away steeply, but nevertheless house a well cairned track which takes a good line through craggy outcrops, leading down to an inviting little scramble. Easy ground follows before the path swings left for a couple of hundred feet of slipping and sliding on extremely loose ground. This soon abates, and the walking proceeds on a rocky path down to the Little Langdale road. Follow the road down its steepest section past Wall End farm to the end of the B5343. After a few yards down the valley turn left over the small bridge to the Old Dungeon Ghyll Hotel. An easy last three quarters of a mile to your start point now remains on the undulating path behind the intake wall after a pilgrimage to the bar of the 'O.D.G'.

Route 13: Gaining Grasmere's High Ground

Walk File

Distance: 13 miles.

Total Ascent: 4550ft.

Start/Finish: Grasmere village.

Terrain: Two contrasting ridges, one of undulating, outcropped ground, the other of generally grassy fells. Steep ascents and descents involved.

Lakeland Maps: OS 1:25000 Outdoor Leisure series NW sheet no.4, NE sheet no. 5 & SE sheet no. 7.

Public Transport: Bus service 555 Lancaster & Kendal – Keswick. Stops Grasmere.

Features visited:

Helm Crag	1299ft
Gibson Knott	1379ft
Calf Crag	1762ft
Steel Fell	1811ft
Fairfield	2863ft
Great Rigg	2513ft
Stone Arthur	1652ft

With its Wordsworthian connections, Grasmere is now firmly established on the itineraries of the many thousands of tourists who come to seek inspiration from its idyllic location. By the same token, the village does not immediately spring to mind as a convenient base for walkers as do say Wasdale Head and Borrowdale. That is not to say worthwhile long walks do not exist from here; on the contrary they do, with a number of high fells within a five or six mile radius. This route takes advantage of their accessibility in combining the east and west ridges of two separate horseshoe walks, namely those of Far Easedale and Fairfield

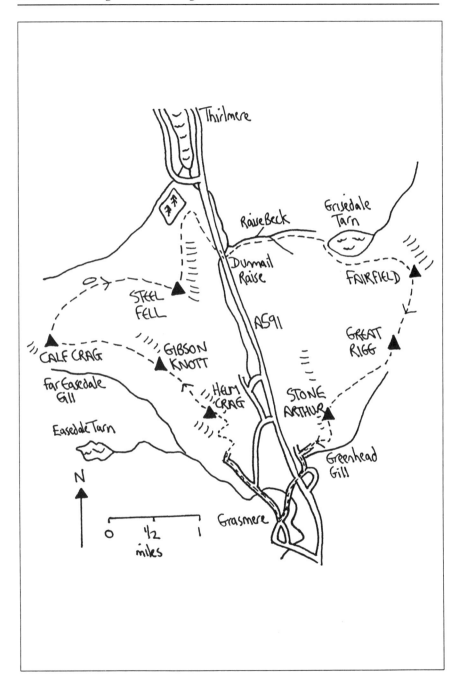

which enclose the A591 on its relentless northward push to the summit of Dunmail Raise.

Leave Grasmere by the Easedale Road, used by those on foot primarily to visit the tarn a couple of miles beyond. After half a mile or so, follow the road round to the right, passing through a gate to continue along the surfaced lane through fields on to the small cluster of houses nestling below Helm Crag. The route's first peak is one of the most, if not the most famous of the Lakeland Fells, and is affectionately known as 'The Lion And The Lamb' after the huge rocks which crown its summit to which they bear a resemblance from the main road. Helm Crag stands at only 1299ft, and is only an hour's walk from the village therefore is climbed by both tourists (who would consider their Lakeland holiday incomplete without at least one peak under their belt) and serious walkers alike. The route to the top has over the years undergone enforced changes of course in an attempt to combat the serious erosion created by the volume of foot traffic pounding its slopes.

Once the tarmac ends, you should keep bearing right to reach the open fell. The ascent is for the most part steep on a well worn path which swings left and right to counter the gradient of the southern flank. After a spell of hard graft you will eventually arrive at a small grass plateau at around the 1000ft contour high above the A591, before the final push through many outcrops to the unique summit. This can be likened to a mini-ridge flanked by a narrow hollow along most of its length, with an unmistakable highest point of an enormous slab of rock unnervingly angled over steep ground. To be able to claim with hand on heart to have reached the very top, you have no option but to tackle it. You may think a fell of this height could not possibly present any difficulties, but do not underestimate this all too brief excursion into the world of rock scrambling.

Having descended gingerly from this impressive monolith, drop down the short steep slope to a small depression to join up with the ridge path which keeps well left of irregular terrain before swinging right to attain Gibson Knott at 1379ft with Harrison Stickle, the biggest of the Langdale Pikes, peeping over the ridge to the southwest. An equally undulating but decidedly boggier little stretch now follows, assisted by cairns to Calf Crag's small top. The main cairn at 1762ft stands at the far end of a craggy platform presiding over the Far Easedale valley.

As previously mentioned, this serrated little three peaked ridge can be part of a high level circuit of Far Easedale with the next objective from

Calf Crag usually being Greenup Edge and then High Raise. Today however, instead of turning for Greenup you should do exactly the opposite and leave the summit to aim for Steel Fell. Immediately from Calf Crag's summit the faintest of tracks heads northwest, missing a large outcrop on its right side, then proceeds to trend northeast along a rolling ridge, past a grouping of small tarns whilst maintaining a line of old iron posts, the remnants of a fence. The improving path soon meets and follows a much newer fence all the way to the summit cairn at 1811ft.

Steel Fell is well off the beaten track and as such suffers from serious neglect at the hands of its better known neighbours. This is a great shame, for there is no finer viewpoint for Thirlmere reservoir which is revealed in almost its entirety stretching away into the distance. As this point virtually overtops the district's most significant geological fault line, a number of the fells 'Back O'Skidda' to the far north are brought into view, not forgetting the Coniston fells to the south. Fence and path remain closely aligned for the beginnings of the descent of the steep north ridge, but where the fence turns sharply right, cross it at a stile to continue on north otherwise you will be in for a very steep drop amongst rough ground which is really too severe for comfort. The slim grass track leads

Thirlmere from Steel Fell

down to an unusual little gate, then swings around to the right along by the intake wall to a gate by the A591.

At Dunmail Raise the main road splits into a short dual carriageway divided by a grass plateau containing a massive pile of stones, allegedly the burial place of King Dunmail after whom the pass takes its name.

The most hair raising part of this walk is getting from one side of the road to the other in one piece, as the dual carriageway offers the first opportunity for some miles for drivers to get the foot down. Many do just this and may not be expecting anyone to be crossing at this bleak location, so take care. Once across, a short roadside walk in the direction of Grasmere will bring you to a further stile, from where you can pick up the excellent path which tracks the course of Raise Beck between Dollywaggon Pike and Seat Sandal, but not before a deserved rest.

The path provides an easy and enjoyable route, emerging at Grisedale Tarn at 1750ft, where it divides. Take the right branch, arcing beneath the slopes of Seat Sandal to reach the col at Grisedale Hause, from where you are faced with the daunting prospect of climbing the huge west face of Fairfield, looking every inch of the 1000ft it measures. As expected, this is a gruelling trudge, as the path has become very unpleasant underfoot. On the steepest and roughest sections two steps forward for every one back is quite normal progress, but you will eventually surface on the summit plateau for the short stroll to the day's highest point, at 2863ft. As you would expect from one of the district's highest fells, Fairfield is a far reaching viewpoint. Numerous cairns exist on this vast summit but the siting of some can lead to confusion, therefore in poor weather reliance on map and compass is essential.

I can clearly recall cycling up from Kendal with a group of friends to tackle my first taste of serious fellwalking as an intrigued teenager. One intrepid character who had even then completed many walks had chosen Fairfield for us. The weather that day was showery but accompanied by a real pea-souper as I was dragged along hating every minute of it and longing to get back to my bike to return home. Put off by the whole experience, I left hillwalking well alone and several years passed before I set foot on the fells again. The weather was awful then too, and continued to be so for perhaps my first dozen or so trips out – I was heavily dependent on W.A. Poucher's magnificent shots in his volume 'The Lakeland Peaks' to display the views, conditions were so bad. Once my luck changed I was at last able to appreciate for myself the scenes he had so faithfully captured on film.

The way ahead now picks up a small section of the horseshoe walk itself. From the main shelter, head due south by a line of cairns for a mile of leisurely grassy walking to Great Rigg. After the ups and downs so far you will hardly notice the short ascent which follows to top its 2513ft summit, from where the tremendous bulk of Fairfield is fully displayed.

In addition to the horseshoe ridge continuing south to Heron Pike and Nab Scar, another pushes southwestward and terminates at the curiously named Stone Arthur. The path to the day's last fell at 1652ft begins at a large cairn soon after departing Great Rigg's top, and follows the line of this broad and easy ridge, necessitating little more than a fifteen minute stroll. The summit cairn sits atop a big boulder amongst a number of small bluffs, part of a band of craggy terrain which indicate the boundaries of Great Rigg's western slopes. Stone Arthur competes with Silver How on the opposite side of the valley for the best bird's eye view of the Grasmere valley, with the village and its lake well seen from both. After Route 20 you can decide for yourself.

The descent begins innocently enough, in a similar vein to the departures from Fairfield and Great Rigg, but the difference here is the progressive steepness of the slope as the path fights gravity to contour effectively through the dense bracken; most definitely one of those 'descent only' routes. The path turns left at a big wall, down to a thin surfaced lane accompanying Greenhead Gill. After bearing left you will eventually join the main road at the Swan Hotel. A short road walk along the B5287 into the centre of Grasmere completes this 'horseshoe within horseshoes'.

Route 14:
The 'Ambleside Round'

Walk File

Distance: 11 miles.

Total Ascent: 3200ft.

Start/Finish: Ambleside.

Terrain: Good paths encountering some rough ground amongst generally grassy fells, with a steep descent to the Kirkstone Pass Inn.

Lakeland Maps: OS 1:25000 Outdoor Leisure series. SE sheet no. 7.

Public Transport: Bus service 555 Lancaster & Kendal – Keswick. Stops Ambleside.

Features visited:

Low Pike	1657ft
High Pike	2155ft
Little Hart Crag	2091ft
Red Screes	2547ft

The majority of circular walks of any reasonable length usually have their beginnings at a farm, hamlet or small village which has become well known as a starting point for the high fells situated close by. Very few walks actually commence directly from a town centre, but having said this I believe you need look no further than Ambleside for an excellent high level circuit. The 'Ambleside Round' takes in a number of fells often climbed either on their own, or as parts of better known routes, and makes for a fine day out with the town as its natural base.

Once in Ambleside, the most convenient place to leave the vehicle is the large car park just off the A591 a hundred yards past one of Lakeland's most popular tourist attractions, the famous Bridge House. Cross the main road to join the Kirkstone Pass road opposite which climbs very steeply out of the town. Take the turning to the left along Sweden Bridge Lane which proceeds to gradually gain height. After the

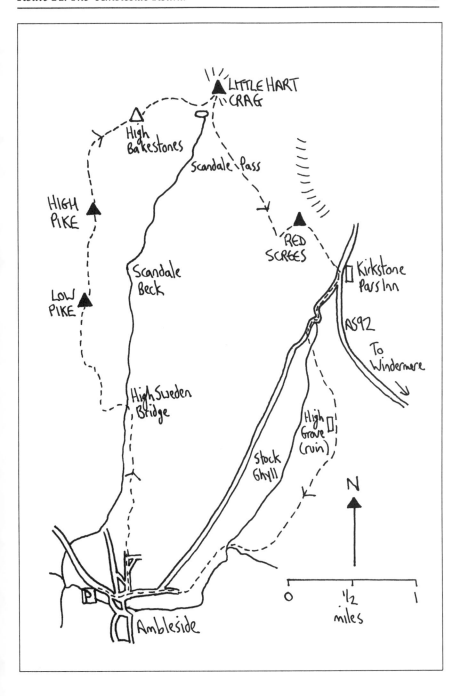

last house, pass through the gate which marks the end of the surfaced road and the beginning of the stony track into the fells. The views westward soon begin to unfold on the pleasant approach to the diminutive High Sweden packhorse bridge spanning Scandale Beck.

Cross the bridge and climb the stile immediately beyond to the open fell-side. Join the path immediately branching left which blazes a trail up the short slope. The route crosses a stile before meeting a more significant track on the extended south ridge of Low Pike, whereupon you will at long last (hopefully) feel progress is being made with the fell now in view beyond a number of small rises. After several more twists and turns to avoid some marshy areas the path meets up with one of the main features of the walk, the extraordinary ridge wall which is quite unrelenting in its progress hugging the most direct line over the highest ground.

The path sticks so closely to the wall in places that helpful use of the rocks along its base enables those who want to keep their feet dry to avoid the worst of the bog. The appearance of cairns usually signifies a summit is not too far away, and here the walking turns quite rough on the final approach to Low Pike's small top at 1657ft. The top stones of the wall actually steal the honour of highest point. As I do not wish to be seen to be the perpetrator of unnecessary damage, you should content yourself with simply laying an achieving hand on top of this most unlikely of summits and taking in a fine retrospective view of Windermere and beyond.

Continue northwards with the wall still at arm's length, beginning with a short descent to a small col from where a complex little ridge of noticeably more rocky terrain stretches out to High Pike. A stile crosses an intervening cross wall which contains an ingenious 'sheep door'. As the going underfoot becomes more awkward, some flexing of the limbs may be required depending on the line you take. Although the wall maintains what has become a rather predictable course along the crest of the ridge, the last few yards sees its partnership with the main path momentarily broken before its eventual renewal at the summit at 2155ft.

Another sizeable expanse of boggy ground has to be circumvented as rock gives way to grass. The next point rising from this extensive land mass is Dove Crag a mile further along the length of the wall (or perhaps I should really say ridge). At an untidy looking pile of stones look out for a faint track leaving the main path on the right, above Thack Bottom Edge. This track becomes more obvious and muddier as it drops down into the upper Scandale valley to the elevated spur of High Bakestones, an airy vantage point topped by an elegant tower of stones worthy of a summit of considerably greater altitude.

The East face of Red Screes

A few cairns offer guidance from High Bakestones aside the east bound track which in parts is no more than the slightest of indentations in the turf. At the point where you become level with a prominent rocky knoll a short way to the right and with Scandale Tarn visible, leave this track left and contour the level ground to meet a line of fence posts marking a major route of descent from Dove Crag to the Scandale Pass. From the fence, pick up the path ahead for an enjoyable scramble to Little Hart Crag, with its two rock tors crowning a most attractive summit. Measuring just over 2000ft (2091ft to be precise) the small top is a fine viewpoint despite being overshadowed by higher fells. With the high level walk above the length of Scandale now completed, retrace your steps to the depression for the track which swings round to its pass.

Dominant from across the depression is Red Screes, which by itself comprises the opposite side of the Scandale valley and hence obliterates any views on the climb of the massive west flank, which is your next objective. A wall runs up from the pass and the path tracks its line for most of the climb before veering east, passing a small summit tarn before the OS column at 2547ft. The column is positioned only a matter of inches from a precipitous slope which plummets down to the Kirkstone Road where the cars and coaches moving tentatively along it are seen to assume Lilliputian proportions.

The all round vista from the summit is quite superb, and in my opinion ranks as one of the very best to be had anywhere in the whole of the district. Looking across Kirkstone, the slender lines of the Kentmere fells are particularly well seen, leading the eye towards and across the High Street plateau and thence anti-clockwise around to the Helvellyn group, the Scafells and the Coniston fells.

Red Screes is a mountain I never tire of, and I always take advantage of the changing seasons to visit it a number of times every year. On those occasions when the weather turns out better than the Met. Office have predicted and as a consequence I have to my regret decided against venturing into the fells, I try to make up for the disappointment with a walk over Cunswick Scar and Scout Scar, two limestone escarpments to the west of Kendal. The sweeping arc of the high Lakeland fells is extremely impressive from 'The Scars', and my eye is usually drawn towards Red Screes' tremendous bulk as I stand envious of those fortunate and intrepid walkers who are at that very moment being rewarded for having seen off the supposedly inclement morning conditions.

Next is an exhilarating descent direct to the Kirkstone Pass. A good track leaves the cairn, soon revealing a bird's eye view of the Inn all of a thousand feet below. There is a steep gully nearby, so keep to the right, and the track which picks its way through the steep ground down to the front door of the Inn, which is Lakeland's highest. During Winter when the snows come the A592 occasionally has to be closed and the Inn thus cut off. Imagine having stayed the night there and waking up in the morning to find yourself snowed in and unable to leave – well if it can't be a day on the fells . . .

The east face of Red Screes is seen at its very best from the summit of the pass, and if you hadn't just completed the descent it is hard to believe there actually is a way down that forbidding incline.

Now begins a pleasurable return walk to civilisation. From the inn, follow the minor road down its initial steep and winding section (known as The Struggle, which was recently included as a climb in the Tour of Britain cycle race) to a gate and signpost for Ambleside. A series of waymarking arrows indicate the way through fields contouring the lower slopes of Wansfell. You will soon come across the ruins of High

Grove, now a sad and derelict place in fine surroundings. The route becomes a wide track, giving over to tarmac in passing through the grounds of The Grove Farm. A better alternative to a lengthy walk along the farm lane presents itself after a couple of minutes walking, where a track heads off right through the small field to a gate and footbridge crossing a youthful Stock Ghyll.

A muddy track leads on to a small wall gap. Once in the field immediately beyond, head for a gate by a barn up ahead. Follow a line of trees into yet another field, then keep close by a large wall curving down to a couple of stiles by High Barn House. The narrow lane passes through a cluster of houses before joining the Kirkstone Pass road and the steep descent into Ambleside for tea and sticky buns.

Route 15: Longsleddale's Lonely Landscape

Walk File

Distance: 12½ miles.

Total Ascent: 3400ft.

Start/Finish: Sadgill Farm, Longsleddale.

Terrain: Extensive moorland on the Eastern ridge, better used paths on rougher ground from Gatescarth Pass onwards.

Lakeland Maps: OS 1:25000 Outdoor Leisure series SE sheet no. 7.

Public Transport: None.

Features visited:

Tarn Crag	2176ft
Branstree	2333ft
Harter Fell	2539ft
Kentmere Pike	2397ft
Shipman Knotts	1926ft

Longsleddale must be one of Lakeland's best kept secrets. It is all too easy, even for the most intrepid hillwalker to be drawn towards the district's 'honeypots' time after time without considering exploring some of the peripheral regions of the district. The next time you're poring over your beloved OS Lakeland maps, I recommend you cast a glance eastward to the fells above this quiet valley which carves its way into the National Park from its boundary at the hamlet of Garnett Bridge, just off the A6 some five miles north of Kendal.

Few houses line the narrow road to its end at to Sadgill farm, whose connection with its surrounding fells is the chosen location for a mountain rescue kit, primarily for the convenience of the Kendal team. A summer evening spent cycling along this beautiful dale from my Kendal home is always time well spent; my only regret is that when I reach the

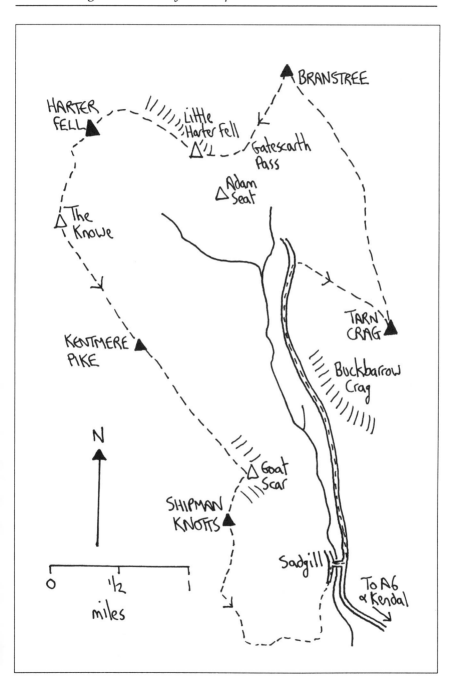

farm, a shortage of available light prevents me from completing the full length of this fine walk which circuits the valley head and in so doing visits five recognised peaks. All is not lost, though; the weekend is never too far away.

Although your start point is Longsleddale, there are inevitably shades of a more famous walk involved, as you follow the eastern ridge of the Kentmere Horseshoe round. Little is revealed of the marked difference of the fells of this ridge from their respective valley floors, with Kentmere displaying extensive grassy flanks, but craggy terrain abounds on the Longsleddale side forming an imposing barrier enclosing the early stages of today's route, the approach to Gatescarth Pass.

Take care not to block any farm gates at Sadgill; there is ample parking for a short way along the unmade old quarry road bounded by substantial stone walls, which makes for an easy start to gain height guiltily. The impressive rock tower up ahead to your right is Buckbarrow Crag, and soon after this is passed, the gradient begins to steepen. Here is a good place for a breather, with the dancing falls of the River Sprint just over the wall to the left. Immediately after passing through the gate towards the top of the Gatescarth 'road', leave it to make your way up the slope to the right for the day's first peak, Tarn Crag. A wall points the way at first, then when it becomes more ruinous, a fence takes up the challenge. An intermittent track of trampled grass attempts to keep the fence close by whilst detouring the numerous irritating marshes which seem to be everywhere. The fence eventually meets another traversing the fell, and at this point you should cross the latter, leaving you a short and pathless walk out across open country up to Tarn Crag's summit.

A small pile of stones indicates the actual highest point at 2176ft, atop a plateau which has a curious looking stone tower fifty yards away at its western extremity. The wooden posts which once were a part of it now float flotsam-like in the small pool at its foot. The apparently meaningless column stands as a monument to the construction of the pipeline from Haweswater reservoir, being one of its survey posts which undoubtedly arouse curiosity when discovered for the first time.

From the surveying tower, the route continues northward, and a path of sorts leaves it towards Branstree, which appears a very long way off across rolling moorland. If you trend right you will meet a directional fence. Keep on its left side until it meets another, presenting a small gap to squeeze through. With the fence now on your left, a vague track can be picked out a short distance away from it, but it is just as easy to make your own route down the broad shoulder of tussocky grass. The flank gradually levels into a small depression just past an unusual 'valley' of peat hags. A gate marks the crossroads for Longsleddale to the west, Shap to the east, and your route, Branstree to the north.

Longsleddale from Goat Scar.

The climb starts uninvitingly, on poorly drained ground. After the accompanying fence finally succumbs, to be replaced by a sturdy wall which spoils any hope of any decent westward views and reducing the walk to Branstree's summit to a pace-counting route march, a test of resolve. The wall ends at a junction with a fence, leaving a narrow gap to gain access to the spacious flat top. Some fifty yards beyond the wall end is the highest point at 2333ft of a few stones, and a low round OS trig station which has the capability to hold sufficient rainwater to serve as a useful bird bath or foot spa. Its sheer flatness makes Branstree's top a real let down as a viewpoint after all you've had to endure to get to it but do not despair, as something in the way of a view can be salvaged by making the short walk to the north east. Here is Artlecrag Pike, a stony crow's nest overseeing a vast moorland ocean.

Branstree marks the end of the east Longsleddale ridge, therefore you should head back for the meeting point of wall and fence to follow the latter for the easy half mile descent to Gatescarth Pass summit. A curious 'L' inscribed on a stone slab can be seen resting against the fence half way down the slope. The summit of Gatescarth Pass proves a convenient lunch stop before tackling Harter Fell rising defiantly opposite.

As the top of the pass is a major turning point for the direct routes of ascent to Harter Fell from Longsleddale and also from Haweswater, the ensuing path which forges up its eastern shoulder displays a fair amount of erosion in marked contrast to the narrow trods and tracks encountered to date. After bypassing Adam Seat the path heads across Little Harter Fell before gradually leaving the edge to accompany yet another fence up to the summit. As the incline begins to diminish the fence takes a sharp change of direction to continue over the highest ground. At this point, the cairn at the 'north top' stands proudly over what is the finest view of Haweswater to be had anywhere in the whole area.

The final approach to Harter Fell is very easy, passing a further prominent cairn along the way, as westward views begin to unfold. The main cairn at 2539ft is the highest point reached on the round, and is a most bizarre structure of rocks and a tangle of iron railings which once stood as the boundary fence. As an all round vantage point Harter Fell is excellent, ranging from the Shap Fells and Pennines to the east to the Coniston and Scafell groups infilling the depressions of the western Kentmere peaks.

The following mile to the next elevation on this easy ridge, Kentmere Pike, is ideal open territory from which to appreciate the scene as you merrily stride along. The path firstly follows the continuing fence across The Knowe, then a wall which combine to link the two summits together, both proving useful guides in poor conditions. A small boggy area in the intervening depression creates a temporary halt to your new found momentum, but this is soon resumed on the easy climb up to Kentmere Pike. An OS column at 2397ft stands on the opposite side of the summit wall which offers no convenient break to reach it, therefore you will have to content yourself with the superb close up of the Yoke – Thornthwaite Crag ridge which is particularly well seen across the Kentmere gap. Not a bad compromise, really.

The day's last fell is Shipman Knotts, a mile further along the ridge, and the only one of the five which does not make the 2000ft mark. The going underfoot is rather spongy in places, but navigable nonetheless. To head direct for Shipman would miss Goat Scar which lies a short way off the main ridge to the east. This rock promontory juts out into the Longsleddale valley almost directly above Sadgill, and as such is an ideal place from which to study both its wildness and its tranquillity in one sweep of the eye. The Scar is easily reached, by following the fence to its corner at a small rise, where it can be crossed leaving a short stroll over to its cairn.

Retrace your steps to the fence corner but this time do not cross back; follow the grass track with the fence now on your right, leaving it when it sweeps left to keep by the fence, down to where it meets a wall. Two stiles need to be climbed in quick succession to negotiate fence and wall to rejoin the main ridge path which leads on to Shipman Knotts. The top of the wall and a cairn on a small outcrop on its opposite side can both stake a claim for the distinction of highest point at 1926ft; there is not much in it, but to me the cairned mound just has it so I will give it the honour.

The return to Sadgill is varied. A good path winds around a grassy knoll on its left side, then crosses a small marshy plateau before dropping steeply to the main Kentmere – Longsleddale bridleway, meeting it at its summit. A gate gives access to the well trodden wide path which drops effortlessly but roughly into the valley on which some repair work has had to be carried out towards the bottom. After a couple more gates the stony path ends at Sadgill's farm outbuildings, leaving a short walk over the picturesque arched bridge to the car; a pleasant end to the day's activities.

Route 16:
Locating Lakes from High Level

Question: When is a lake not a lake? Answer: When it's a 'mere' or a 'water', spawning the old wives' tale that there is really only one lake in the Lake District, and that is Bassenthwaite Lake.

If this walk took things so literally it would last little more than a few minutes. Instead it follows a route over well known and less frequented peaks and passes from where no less than eighteen major lakes can be seen, either in whole or in part, along with a myriad of tarns in the bargain. Coupled with the prospect of walking across Lakeland in two days, an appetising adventure awaits.

Walk File

Distance: 15¼ miles (Day One), 12¾ miles (Day Two).

Total Ascent: 3600ft (Day One), 4850ft (Day Two).

Start: Car Park, Mardale Head, Haweswater.

Finish: Honister Pass, or Seatoller. Overnight Stop: Grasmere.

Terrain: On grassy fells at first, becoming increasingly rougher with westward progress. A number of steep ascents and descents involved during the two days.

Lakeland Maps: OS 1:25000 Outdoor Leisure series NE sheet no. 5 and SE sheet no. 7 (Day One). NW sheet no.4, SW sheet no. 6 & SE sheet no. 7 (Day Two).

Public Transport: Nothing to Mardale Head. (Bus service 555 Lancaster & Kendal – Keswick. Stops at Grasmere). Bus service 79 (The Borrowdale Bus) Keswick – Seatoller.

Day One

Features visited:

Kidsty Pike	2560ft
Rampsgill Head	2581ft
The Knott	2423ft
Seat Sandal	2415ft

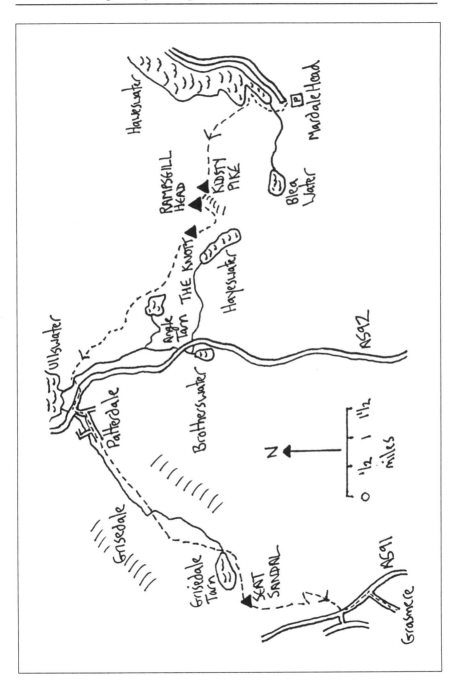

The walk begins at the car park at the head of the valley alongside Haweswater, the highest of the large lakes at just short of 800ft above sea level. The assistance of an understanding driver will be required, as no public transport is available to here. The path to the high fells rounds the head of the reservoir and leads on past the delightful wooded peninsula of The Rigg, which once presided over the now drowned village of Mardale. On two occasions in recent years the water level has been drawn down to such an extent that the pasture walls and the foundations of the dismantled buildings have reappeared defiantly from their watery grave. I among many others was drawn to witness this eerie sight first hand, yet standing there on the valley floor invoked feelings of sadness for the community who were forced to leave their beloved valley.

The path passes through an old sheepfold, then between two lines of stones to cross Riggindale Beck at a footbridge. Immediately before crossing a second bridge, turn left up the slope to pick up a grassy path towards the first landmark, Kidsty Pike. The grass gives way to a rough track, climbing through a rocky gully out onto the open ridge. The now wide path on gently rising slopes provides an easy route to the small peaked top at 2560ft, sitting as close as it could be to a fearsome plunge into Riggindale. If luck is on your side you may catch sight of one of the valley's resident golden eagles.

The High Street group, of which Kidsty Pike is a part, provide fast walking territory with far reaching views which are Pennine as much as they are Lakeland. As the individual tops are of similar height, the ridges linking them are very straightforward, with that from Kidsty Pike to Rampsgill Head perhaps the least demanding of them all. A small diversion from the blazed trail is required to reach the highest point situated at 2581ft.

On departing Rampsgill Head, the main path tracks the course of the old Roman road. When you reach the depression at the Straits of Riggindale, head north to follow the broken wall which swings left to ascend the short flank of The Knott to its enormous cairn at 2423ft. Its western slopes are quite different in falling away steeply to Hayeswater, an unfrequented lake off the beaten track in an austere setting. Keep the wall close by on your left for an easy descent to rejoin the main High Street – Patterdale path at a further cairn. The first couple of miles on the way to Angle Tarn are hideously boggy after rain, but the path does become firmer in its latter stages down to Patterdale village, and lunch.

Next comes a very fine walk up the Grisedale valley which is enclosed by a number of imposing peaks. From Patterdale, follow the main A592 past the village church and turn first left onto a surfaced lane, the beginning of the Striding Edge route to Helvellyn. After around a mile the way to the Edge bears right, with your route directly ahead. The farm road eventually becomes a well used track which climbs by Grisedale Beck directly to the outflow of Grisedale Tarn. This is an impressive sheet of water which could quite easily pass for a small lake, given its considerable surface area. It is also one of Lakeland's deepest tarns.

St. Sunday Crag & Grisedale Tarn from Seat Sandal.

Continue along the shoreline to Grisedale Hause, a small col between Fairfield and Seat Sandal, the latter the next and final top of this first day. The climb is short but hard work, and alongside a gravity-defying wall. The slope soon gives way to easier terrain towards the summit cairn, a well made pile of stones at 2415ft. This outpost of the Helvellyn group is a rewarding ascent in itself offering outstanding views (from the summit and the smaller southwest cairn) of lakes, tarns and mountains. The first day is completed by a descent of the south ridge to Grasmere, somewaht prolonged due to an enforced directional change at the intake wall. The village has a wide range of comfortable accommodation where you can recharge your batteries for the day ahead.

Day Two

Features visited:

Sergeant Man	2414ft
High Raise	2500ft
Great Gable	2949ft
Green Gable	2628ft
Brandreth	2344ft
Grey Knotts	2287ft

Opposite the village green, a sign set in a wall indicates the road to be followed, that to Easedale Tarn. After around half a mile when the road turns to the right, leave it to enter the small wood ahead crossing Easedale Beck by a small stone bridge. An established route passes through fields, man-made for a good part of the climb, with the cascading waters of Sour Milk Gill a focus of attention.

Before long, Easedale Tarn comes into view, set in a massive corrie backed by imposing craggy outcrops. Press on into the corrie on an undulating and narrowing track which climbs its way through a natural break in the defences of the steepening slopes to another shelf of level ground, passing the smaller Codale Tarn before linking up with another distinct path rising out of the Great Langdale valley. Follow this north-westwards to the small summit of Sergeant Man at 2414ft, a fine all round vantage point, particularly for the formidable cliff of Pavey Ark and the unmistakable Langdale Pikes in the near distance.

The way ahead now lies due west, however this bearing would miss out on High Raise, the easiest of half mile northwestwards continuations. In clear conditions, the slight advantage in altitude the fell has over its near neighbours guarantees an outstanding view from its OS column at 2500ft, including a glimpse through the fells of a couple of northern lakes obscured thus far, one quite distinct, the other only the tiniest of sections seen below the Skiddaw massif.

You can now aim southwest to join an intermittent track for the head of the Stake Pass. After two further miles the route merges with the Rossett Gill track at the second Angle Tarn in two days, their cumulative width combining as a single thoroughfare up to Esk Hause. This major arterial route provides access to England's highest group of fells.

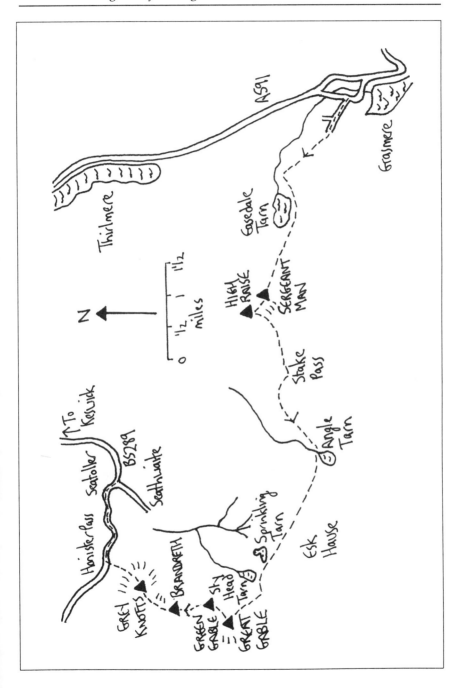

After leaving the cross wall shelter which has provided much refuge over the years, it is downhill past Sprinkling Tarn, one of the highest of the larger tarns and reputedly the wettest place in the country with in excess of an incredible ten feet per year. Be prepared therefore to don the kagoule & leggings as you press on beneath the towering cliffs of Great End onto another major Lakeland crossroads, the Sty Head Pass.

I would advise a good few minutes rest here, for a very steep and rough 1500ft climb is next in store to attain the revered summit of Great Gable. Unfortunately this is achieved by way of an extremely eroded trench and as such is a hard slog. Nevertheless, it offers the most direct route up from the pass and it is several hours now since your leg muscles were last stretched by an uphill section of any note. It is also the final substantial climb of the two days.

Although this slope seems interminable, eventually it does peter out leaving a short walk across the summit dome to the highest point at 2949ft. From this celebrated viewpoint you will not begrudge the energy expended on that river of stone and scree now well and truly behind you as you savour the exceptional full length view of Wastwater and its remarkable screes. A superlative to adequately describe this scene has yet to be discovered.

A knee jerking descent now follows down Gable's northeast shoulder to Windy Gap, appropriately named as you will find out. After a short climb to Green Gable at 2628ft, the ridge before you is broad and without difficulty. The path branching left aims for the first of two prominent rises, namely Brandreth, therefore at the point where a line of fence posts can be seen up ahead, follow the latter to attain the 2344ft summit, and a short way beyond, Grey Knotts at 2287ft. Both these fells are excellent viewpoints for the western lakes and the mountain ranges dividing them. An easy but steep descent bearing slightly east of north now remains, never too far from a guiding fence, down to the youth hostel at the top of the Honister Pass. This is a very convenient overnight stop, but if you have made other arrangements you will need to walk a further mile or so down the pass to the hamlet of Seatoller for the Borrowdale bus to Keswick, with ten summits and eighteen lakes (Haweswater, Hayeswater, Ullswater, Brothers Water, Windermere, Coniston Water, Grasmere, Thirlmere, Esthwaite Water, Rydal Water, Elterwater, Derwent Water, Bassenthwaite Lake, Wastwater, Ennerdale Water, Buttermere, Crummock Water and Loweswater) under your belt.

Route 17: Hall To Hall

Walk File

Distance: 10¼ miles.

Total Ascent: 3450ft.

Start: Cow Bridge, off A592 (GR 403133, OS 2½" map, NE sheet).

Finish: Kentmere Hall (GR 451042, OS 2½" map, SE sheet).

Terrain: A number of steep gradients involving some rough climbs, following well used paths.

Lakeland Maps: OS 1:25000 Outdoor Leisure series NE sheet no. 5 and SE sheet no. 7.

Public Transport: Bus service 517 Bowness – Glenridding. Mountain Goat Bus Windermere – Glenridding (From Tourist Information Centre). Bus service 519 Windermere – Kentmere (Experimental service Summer 1994).

Features visited:

Caudale Moor	2502ft
Thornthwaite Crag	2569ft
Froswick	2359ft
Ill Bell	2476ft
Yoke	2309ft

I believe the enquiring mind of the hillwalker is not simply focussed on things geological, meteorological or cartographical when other features of interest can be appreciated during the course of a day's expedition. The Lake District contains a number of historical buildings, and on this linear route two of its finest examples can be seen, namely Hartsop Hall at its beginning and Kentmere Hall at its end, separated by a distance of only six miles as the crow flies. Both are situated in exquisite surroundings with an appetising group of fine peaks in between. It should be noted that public transport here is extremely limited, justifying the use of two cars or better still a friendly driver.

The walk starts from the Hartsop end, but not directly at the door of its Hall. Instead convenient use is made of the usually busy car park at

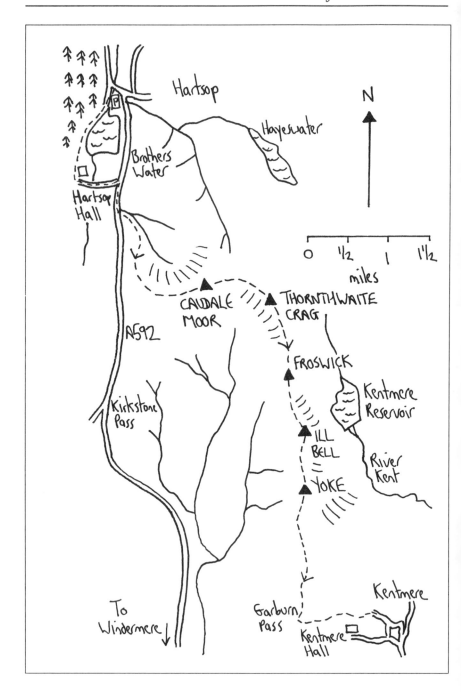

Cow Bridge just off the A592 half a mile further north. From here you can follow a well made path through the lower slopes of Low Wood at the base of the Hartsop Above How ridge. This is a very easy and enjoyable start to the day along the shoreline of the mysterious Brotherswater towards Hartsop Hall and the magnificent skyline of peaks surrounding the Kirkstone Pass.

Brotherswater and Ullswater from the slopes of Caudale Moor.

The first dwelling on this site, which is recognised as the oldest in the valley, is believed to have been in existence in the twelfth century when the valley was a part of a Norman hunting forest. The Hall itself took its name from the Hartsop family some four hundred years later, having been rebuilt in the fifteenth century. The whole estate (including Brotherswater) was acquired by the National Trust in 1947.

From the farm, pick up the lane up to the Brotherswater Inn by the side of the A592. A spot of road walking is now required, but thankfully for only a short distance until Caudale Bridge is reached. Cross the bridge, then leave the road at a gate on your left to gain access to the extensive northwest ridge, which is one of several fine routes to the top of Caudale Moor. The well used path initially climbs alongside a wall above Caudale Beck on a green path through bracken.

Further up the slope the path passes through a gap in the now collapsed wall, and soon after turns sharp left in a narrow channel. Be sure to make the short diversion to the ghostly ruins of the Caudale quarry buildings perched high above the valley. A small ring of rocks on a grassy level indicate somebody's inspired choice for a wild camp, and just above this, a latticework of iron posts cover the entrance to a perilous shaft. The quarrymen would undoubtedly have thought highly of the excellent views from their place of work, back into Patterdale and ahead into the mountain's very own corrie.

A couple of fair paths strike up the slope from the quarries to meet the narrow ridge. A solitary cairn stands at the end of the incline, revealing a vast summit expanse of grass and isolated rocks. A thin trod passes close by a couple of tarns, and heads for a wall to join up with the path from the top of the Kirkstone Pass, Caudale Moor's easiest route of ascent in having a 1500ft start. Just beyond a further collapsed wall is the summit itself at 2502ft, named Stony Cove Pike and marked by a sizeable cairn.

A seemingly straightforward walk to reach the fells beyond is denied by the intervening col of Threshthwaite Mouth. A rough track leaves the summit in the direction of Hartsop Dodd, Caudale's northern shoulder, but quickly swings east and picks its way down the rocky slope alongside a ruined wall, descending to the col. Here is a most welcome resting place, for it is now all uphill from here to Thornthwaite Crag.

The steep section of this mile long connecting ridge is one of the most exasperating to be found anywhere, and can be likened to ascending on a down escalator of scree in places. When the stony ground eventually relents, an enjoyable stroll on a much easier gradient is left alongside a solid summit wall, to the massive pillar of stones at 2569ft. This is a well known landmark which is clearly visible with the naked eye from a distance of several miles. As a viewpoint, Thornthwaite Crag ranks highly which I suppose really goes without saying, as you would expect nothing less when in the presence of such a cairn.

Thornthwaite Crag is slightly set back from the natural lines which comprise the Kentmere Horseshoe round, hence a distinct offshoot path has developed to its summit. It is this path which you should now follow to the south to join up with the main ridge, but do not make the mistake of being on the one which trends to the right. This is the course of the old

Roman Road which traverses the grassy flanks of Froswick and Ill Bell to the Troutbeck valley. Your path keeps strictly to the watershed, hugging the edge of the escarpment above Froswick's rugged east flank. The final few feet can be bypassed on its right side if so desired, but the short final climb to the summit is too tempting to warrant this detour. From this exposed vantage point at 2359ft, you can marvel at an absorbing aerial view of Kentmere Reservoir and into the depths of Hall Cove, the birthplace of Kendal's river Kent.

The route continues over the summit and descends steeply to another small depression. From here it is also possible to avoid the next summit by taking the track to the west, but all this achieves is to miss out on the excellent Ill Bell, famous for its three long-established cairns, now down to two at the time of writing. The final serious climb of the day is short but tiring on eroded terrain bringing you to the summit at 2476ft, a remarkably similar but slightly larger scale version of the neighbouring Froswick. Ill Bell has all the attributes of the perfect mountain form, with steep gradients dominating all sides, a most impressive sight from its near neighbours. The eastern and western flanks fall away in a sheer plunge to their respective valleys of Kentmere and Troutbeck. You can almost take it for granted there will be a superb view from the summit, and true to form, it does not disappoint. Many of Lakeland's finest, make up the western horizon, along with a sweeping view down Windermere to the south.

As I often find myself looking towards the Ill Bell ridge on a clear day during my lunch hour from the office in Kendal, it makes a pleasant change to be able to look back towards the town every once in a while. To be amongst these fells in the warmth of the evening summer sun and observe the dramatic shadows cast by their graceful outlines is an unforgettable experience.

Having seen all there is to see from Ill Bell, a short steep descent follows to gain the broad south ridge for an easy mile above the incline of Star Crag to the final summit of the day. The large cairn which indicates the summit of Yoke at 2309ft stands alongside what is now generally recognised as the main path, which has superseded yet another westward lying track detouring the highest point of the fell.

Yoke's eastern summit slopes fall away in the sheer face of Rainsbarrow Crag leaving a southward continuation as the only feasible route of descent to Kentmere in the direction of the Garburn Pass. At a wall corner a short way down the eroded slope, alternative routes present themselves, with the best used crossing the large stile to keep the wall on the left before trending away from it to avoid marshy terrain just above the head of the pass. A more complex variation in terms of navigation and not marked on the 2½" OS map, does not cross the wall but gradually slants left, eventually picking up the standard way back to Kentmere via an easy gully.

The Garburn 'road' makes for a straightforward descent into the Kentmere valley. Pass between the farm buildings at its terminus to join the surfaced road leading down to the village. Just beyond the old church a short way down the signposted Ings lane stands Kentmere Hall with its impressive pele tower of the fourteenth century. Towers of this type are understood to have been constructed as a defence against raiding parties. Kentmere Hall was once home to the Gilpin family who had the dubious honour of slaying the last boar in the district.

Kentmere is only a small village and places of refreshment are very few and far between, therefore celebrating another day's achievements may have to be postponed until Staveley is reached, a further 3½ mile walk down the valley and a stop on the Keswick – Kendal bus route and the Windermere – Oxenholme Lakes rail line.

Route 18:
Discovering Deepdale Fells

Walk File

Distance: 11¼ miles.

Total Ascent: 3450ft.

Start/Finish: Patterdale village.

Terrain: Good paths throughout on grassy ridges, with some rough ground.

Lakeland Maps: OS 1:25000 Outdoor Leisure series NE sheet no. 5.

Public Transport: Bus service 517 Bowness – Glenridding. Stops Patterdale. Service 108 Penrith – Patterdale. Mountain Goat Bus Windermere – Glenridding. Stops Patterdale. (From Tourist Information Centre).

Features visited:

Birks	2040ft
St. Sunday Crag	2756ft
Fairfield	2863ft
Hart Crag	2698ft
Hartsop Above How	1870ft

The land which lies immediately to the west of the A592 between Kirkstone Pass and the head of Ullswater contains no less than three smaller 'tributary' valleys, namely Dovedale, Grisedale and Deepdale. The latter possesses spectacular rock scenery, with its upper reaches confined by the cliffs of Fairfield and Hart Crag and the steep flanks of St. Sunday Crag. Add Birks and Hartsop Above How at either end and you have a five-peak round trip above this most compact and impressive of valleys.

Just beyond Patterdale church in the direction of Glenridding, follow the narrow surfaced lane climbing gradually out of the village, the popular start for Helvellyn. After half a mile you will come across a signpost by a gate on the left. At this point leave the lane, and those

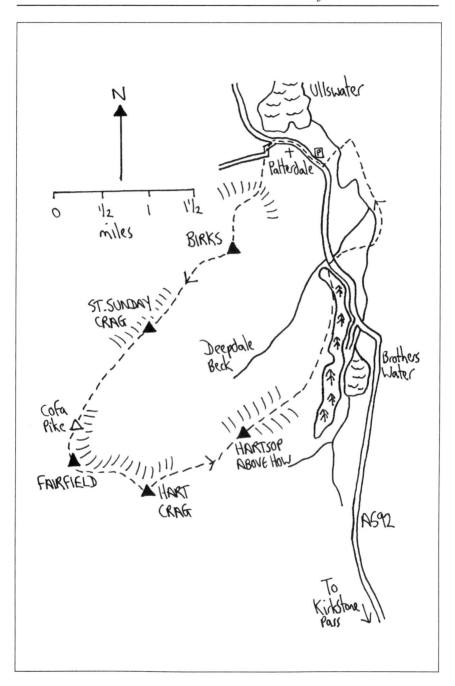

getting on with their walk to Grisedale Tarn, or assault of Striding Edge (covered next in Route 19), to begin the day's first ascent. It is a steep one, starting on a rough track which swings round to a further gate and stile at a small cluster of trees, to open up the steepening lower slopes of Birks.

At a small rise you are confronted by a sizeable wall. At this point the path turns sharp left to avoid having to cross it straight away, this achieved further up at a small gap filled by another wooden stile, at Thornhow End, the northernmost edge of a curved flank of crags. The views back to Ullswater from this favourite halt are as beautiful as any to be had elsewhere.

The path cuts a pronounced groove in Birks' northern flank. At a cairn situated on a small grass plateau, leave the main route skirting the fell by aiming directly for St. Sunday Crag, to bear left on grass then rock. This track has a few cairns along the way and takes a number of directional changes before at last gaining the summit ridge and clear sight of a small pile of stones that marks Birks' highest point at 2040ft, now devoid of OS column. The views from here are well worth taking in before departing for St. Sunday Crag itself.

The route now continues across the grassy top and drops down to a small depression to rejoin the aforementioned 'bypass' path. A steepish ascent then ensues, proceeding obliviously above an extremely precipitous northwest face of rock gullies and buttresses containing the infamous Pinnacle ridge which only experienced scramblers should tackle. In view of the exposure factor with the Grisedale valley far, far below, this is unquestionably a scramble for the connoisseur.

A very wide shale-like path complete with cairns crosses the uppermost slopes, necessitating an easy but drawn out walk to the summit cairn at 2756ft. This is a truly fine mountain viewpoint, sandwiched between the long ridges of the Helvellyn and High Street groups, completed by the Scafells conveniently filling the Grisedale Tarn 'gap' on the horizon. Speaking of sandwiches, here is as good a place as any to sample your early morning culinary endeavours whilst contemplating what I can describe without hesitation as a superb approach to attain the celebrated Fairfield.

The beginnings of this section of the route are straightforward enough, across the remainder of the summit plateau along a good path descending the long grassy southwest ridge to Deepdale Hause, Fairfield appearing ever more forbidding from the steepening angle of view as you lose height. The col is the lowest point of the connecting ridge, however the ascent which immediately follows does not take place on Fairfield itself, but on the intervening pinnacle of Cofa Pike, which always seems much bigger than it really is. The climb entails an enjoyable rocky scramble to defeat its rocky cone, at the same time clearing the way ahead for the climb to the day's highest ground. From Cofa's large cairn worthy of individual mountain status the views across upper Deepdale above a nasty drop, to Fairfield's buttressed northern face are quite stupendous. This is a well liked line of approach and as a consequence the walking is rough on unstable stony ground. It can prove an awkward climb up to the point where the gradient eases at Fairfield's ungainly looking but effective cross wall shelter and summit cairn a handful of yards distant. With an extensive network of crags only a matter of yards away, this flat and exposed top is not one on which to randomly wander in poor weather. If conditions are with you, from 2863ft above sea level the fell will duly oblige as a fine vantage point. The sheer immensity of the summit plateau does regrettably obscure some of its near neighbours, thus restricting a good sight of its radiating 'horseshoe' ridges.

The Helvellyn group from Fairfield.

A line of regularly spaced cairns leaves the summit southeastward lining the wide path which proceeds to swing still further left, and in doing so keeps to the easy ground high above the abyss. A steepish descent on rugged ground reaches Link Hause, leaving a rough climb to Hart Crag's summit cairn, which I recently noticed had been precariously elevated by the addition of a number of individual stones piled one on top of the other. I concluded somebody must have been ticking off all Lakeland's 2700ft plus tops, and had wished to extend their list with a 'new-style' Hart Crag, promoting it from its accredited height of 2698ft.

The main cairn lies at the far end of a short summit ridge of rocky outcrops. Etched in my memory is a whistle-stop visit to Hart Crag several years ago as a 'competitor' in the Fairfield Horseshoe fell race. One fair Sunday morning two of us had set off for Rydal intent simply to walk the round, but on arriving discovered an unexpectedly crowded scene; the official race was taking place. Carried along by the wave of enthusiasm, we decided to enter.

I thought I was pretty fit at the time until that race got underway. I was gasping for breath even before the first ascent, such was the electrifying pace set by the rest of the field. On leaving a typically gale buffeted Fairfield bound for Hart Crag I can clearly remember looking back and seeing absolutely nobody; I was convinced I was last, but was too exhausted to go any faster. Several walkers along the way offered encouraging words; what I would have given to have swapped places with them. Somehow I managed to get through the remaining miles and back into Rydal, even overtaking one or two compatriots, delighting at my time of two hours and one second. I considered this more than respectable, until I discovered 386 people had already finished.

From Hart Crag, you now need to leave the blazed trail to head northeast, to join a prominent sweeping ridge whose highest point is commonly known as Hartsop Above How. The path descends swiftly, negotiating a rugged section at the boundary of the Fairfield crag complex to gain the ridge proper, after which the walking becomes easy on grass. As you progress along what becomes a quite worn path which incidentally avoids the final few feet, steep slopes are all the time building on either side to create a neat and airy top, sadly anonymous on the 1¼" OS map. Dividing Dovedale and Deepdale, the fell opens up an interesting perspective into both valleys.

From the summit, climb back down to the main path for the continuation of the hummocked ridge and begin the long descent into the Patterdale valley. Soon after a large gap in the rock at the top of Gill Crag (a small 'window' in the crag wall high above Dovedale) the grassy ridge begins to widen with the path meeting a wall rising across its southern slopes. Path and wall curve northward together, and even after another wall is crossed, a signpost immediately opposite instructs you do not deviate from your long-followed line.

The wall eventually falls away from the path, to be replaced by a fence. A stile some thirty yards along the fence gives access into the tree covered lower reaches of Deepdale Park. By keeping left you next cross yet another wall and out into open fields where a traditional red telephone box by the A592 soon comes into view.

A toilsome last mile back to Patterdale along the road can be avoided, but I should point out slightly lengthened, by an interesting diversion along the base of the fells which lie on the opposite side of the valley. Only fifty yards along the road over Deepdale Bridge turn right at a Public Bridleway signpost. The route heads through fields, then crosses Goldrill Beck and bears left along a well- used track for a nearly tarmac-free mile. Turn back 'inland' towards Patterdale and finally recross the beck at Goldrill Bridge into the village where the White Lion Inn beckons to round off another splendid day's outing.

Route 19:
Edging around Helvellyn

Walk File

Distance: 9 miles.

Total Ascent: 3050ft.

Start/Finish: Glenridding village.

Terrain: On well used paths throughout, including two exposed scrambles.

Lakeland Maps: OS 1:25000 Outdoor Leisure series NE sheet no. 5.

Public Transport: Bus service 517 Bowness – Glenridding Service 108 Penrith – Patterdale. Stops Glenridding. Mountain Goat Windermere – Glenridding (From Tourist Information Centre).

Features visited:

Birkhouse Moor	2356ft
Helvellyn	3118ft
Catstycam	2917ft

Despite giving up a mere ninety two feet to England's highest mountain, Helvellyn has the distinction of being the country's most popular 3000ft peak, the highest point of an immense high level watershed. Both the main A591 and A592 roads offer convenient access to numerous challenging routes of ascent, nearly all of which nowadays suffer under the pressure of stampedes of walking boots. To undertake a full traverse of the hill reveals on the one hand, benign western slopes where sheep happily graze, whereas to the east, a supreme work of art displaying the forces of glaciation in the shape of the aretes of Swirral and Striding Edges enclosing Red Tarn in a vast bowl. To have the opportunity to set foot on such spectacular terrain proves an unforgettable experience, one many return for on a regular basis.

Best for parking is the large Lake District National Park car park at Greenside Road, from the back of which Helvellyn is signposted. Follow

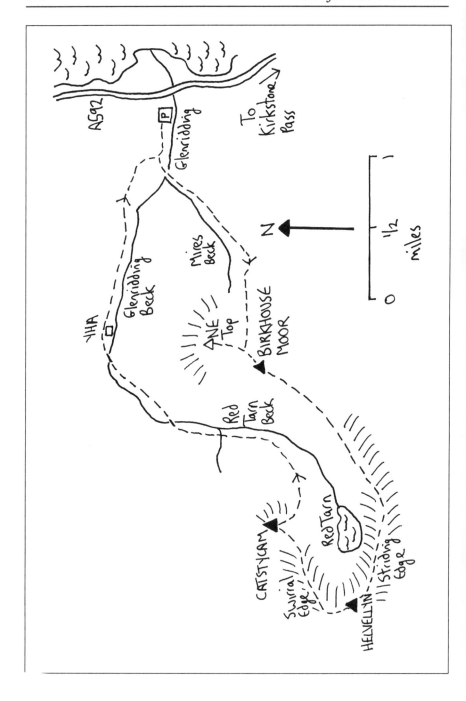

the road up the hill passing the Travellers Rest pub, and where the road splits, with clear signposts again pointing the way, head left to cross Rattlebeck Bridge where the climbing begins, on a wide stony path which ultimately brings you to a gate at a wall corner with the open fell-side of Birkhouse Moor rising defiantly before you. The level path immediately ahead contours its base in heading for Red Tarn, but your route to the summit of this unfrequented fell begins by bearing left to pick up the well-used path climbing alongside Mires Beck, now the only legitimate route from Glenridding as the way up Birkhouse Moor's northeast flank is now out of bounds, blocked off by a couple of wooden barriers.

On Striding Edge

The climb is a good one for the day's first as there are no problems *en route*, presenting a quick way onto the long ridge culminating in Helvellyn's summit. The path passes a circular sheepfold, meeting up with a wall on the left. The route is forced away from the line of the wall at an erosion control sign, and proceeds to maintain a course marked out by a series of posts traversing the slope. At a junction of paths it is well worth detouring sharply right to almost double back on yourself, in order to stride out across the grassy expanse to a prominent cairn at the top of the aforementioned northeast ridge route, from where Ullswater is quite resplendent.

I should state this cairn is not the actual summit of Birkhouse Moor, but do not consider this easiest of diversions as a wasted journey as here is a location finer than that of the true highest point which is to be gained half a mile further along the ridge in the direction of Helvellyn. Rather like Caw Fell in Route 7, the summit cairn proper of Birkhouse Moor at 2356ft lies a few yards beyond a kink in the ridge wall. The east face of Helvellyn fringed by its prodigious double edges will transfix your gaze, and justifiably so; it is an remarkable feature.

Birkhouse Moor's southern flank possesses the exhaustively trodden Helvellyn 'highway' from Patterdale, whose understandable popularity as a fine approach has been its very undoing in creating a sad blot on a fine mountain landscape. The Mires Beck and the Patterdale paths converge at the famous Hole in the Wall, even named as such on the 2½" OS map. The wall gap has become a common stopping-off place for groups to gather, sharing lunch and excitable discussion in eager anticipation of an impending assault on Striding Edge.

The ground progressively narrows and roughens, and eventually peaks into the Edge itself. Your next quarter mile is one of the most spectacular you could wish for, along a slender ridge of jutting rock buttresses, high above steep drops on both sides. To traverse the crest throughout its length gives a thrill of real exposure which should not be taken lightly, as it takes a strong nerve to maintain any semblance of a recognisable gait for the whole trip. One or two small climbs require the use of hands and feet, however an easier option is available by following the clear narrow track just down from the top which keeps mostly to the Red Tarn side.

Progress can be very slow on balmy Summer days which bring out hillwalkers in droves, determined to fulfil an ambition. Here is one of the few places on the hills where enforced queuing may be the order of the day; a toll gate at either end would no doubt raise sufficient funds for years of future footpath maintenance. Far fetched yes, but who would begrudge a quid for such entertainment. These days good Winter conditions hardly seem to reduce volumes with hillwalking now an established year round activity, but this straightforward scramble as far as scrambles go can be rapidly transformed into a serious undertaking, as is the neighbouring Swirral. Far too many column inches sadly have to be given over each year in the local paper to reporting tragic incidents occurring on this particular ridge walk.

The sting in the tail of this marvellous traverse is a troublesome ten foot climb down to the small col attaching the Edge to Helvellyn itself. This reminds me of once having to wait patiently at this point a few years ago behind a couple of fellow walkers one at the top, one at the bottom, embroiled in the onerous task of man-handling their pet sheepdog (who was having none of it) down the climb. Somehow between them they managed it, and the dog charged on to beat everyone hands down up the slope opposite.

Hillwalkers of the two legged kind do not usually attack this imposing flank with such gusto, instead preferring to dwell on what has just been conquered during the steady plod to the summit. The steep rocky gradient which has become very eroded soon lessens into an extensive high level plateau. In emerging by the Gough Memorial stone overlooking Striding Edge, you should now swing right to follow the rim of the massive escarpment to make the triumphant stroll up to Helvellyn's solid cross wall shelter. The hill is home to many sheep, and those who choose to venture as far as these uppermost expanses are a merciless bunch who will be off with your rations in the blinking of an eye, so be on your guard.

Although you would expect the summit to be occupied by the usual hordes of hillwalkers and mountain bikers (and sheep), it has been the scene of some unusual events, from landing an aircraft to the vending of tea from an urn carried by a spirited hillgoer to swell the coffers of local Mountain Rescue teams. Doubtless enough material exists amongst the hillwalking fraternity for collation into a 'Tales From Helvellyn' publication.

A hundred yards beyond the wall shelter stands the OS column overlooking the steep plunge into Red Tarn. Being the highest ground for miles around at all of 3118ft, an almost incalculable mass of fells are clearly visible in every direction, a panorama of both quality and quantity which warrants detailed analysis. The summit has also become a magnet for observing the sunrise on the longest day.

Continue northwestwards to maintain the edge of the cliffs for a short way, until the distinct path chooses to suddenly descend at a big cairn and follow a rocky tract which soon merges into Swirral Edge. Shorter than its more illustrious 'partner', it too has a crest-avoiding lower track. Take the left fork of the dividing path as this proceeds to climb the steep grassy flank up to the summit of Catstycam's tiny peak at 2917ft. From here the route so far can be easily traced in retrospect, and in so doing you can observe the slow moving procession of a silhouetted human chain on Striding Edge across the corrie.

A fair track leaves Catstycam on its crag-free east side, but diminishes with the loss of height. As the steep ridge begins to ease just below the outflow of Red Tarn, the route bends northwards to descend into upper Glenridding on an at first muddy path passing the delightful falls of Red Tarn Beck. The beck is crossed at a wooden footbridge by a sheepfold where it merges into a wider Glenridding Beck. To complete one of the very finest of Lakeland's circuitous routes, cross the beck lower down via the small footbridge over a weir, to reach the disused Greenside lead mine and further on, the superbly sited Youth Hostel, to pick up the Greenside 'road' back down to the village.

Route 20: In Search of Dry Land on The Central Ridge

Walk File

Distance: 19¼ miles.

Total Ascent: 4200ft.

Start: A591 at signpost for Walla Crag (GR 287227, OS 2½" map, NW sheet).

Finish: Ambleside.

Terrain: Some long stretches of marshy ground, but generally on good paths and tracks.

Lakeland Maps: OS 1:25000 Outdoor Leisure series NW sheet no.4, SW sheet no. 6 & SE sheet no. 7.

Public Transport: Bus service 555 Lancaster & Kendal – Keswick. Stops Ambleside.

Features visited:

Walla Crag	1234ft
Bleaberry Fell	1932ft
High Seat	1996ft
High Tove	1665ft
Ullscarf	2370ft
High Raise	2500ft
Sergeant Man	2414ft
Blea Rigg	1776ft
Silver How	1292ft
Loughrigg Fell	1099ft

The terrain of this linear route is as diverse as you could hope to find in Lakeland, from striding out on firm well trodden paths to picking your way through marshland in a determined attempt to keep your feet dry. Do not be deterred at the prospect of encountering ground which has above average water retaining properties but instead make sure you have packed a spare pair of socks (just in case), and look forward to

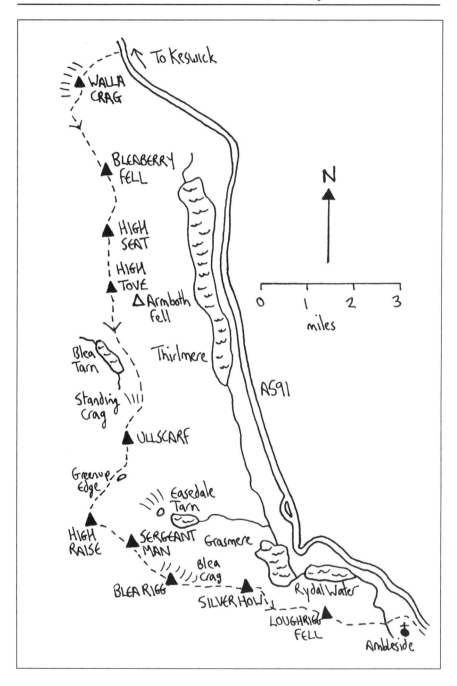

To Keswick

WALLA CRAG

BLEABERRY FELL

HIGH SEAT

HIGH TOVE

△Armboth Fell

N

0   1   2   3
miles

Blea Tarn

Thirlmere

Standing Crag

A591

ULLSCARF

Greenup Edge

Easedale Tarn

HIGH RAISE

SERGEANT MAN

Grasmere

Blea Crag

BLEA RIGG

SILVER HOW

Rydal Water

LOUGHRIGG FELL

Ambleside

visiting no fewer than ten recognised tops, which as individual fells differ considerably in popularity.

The car can be left in Ambleside to take advantage of public transport (service bus to Keswick) in order to tackle the walk north to south. The starting point is by the A591 just before it descends steeply into Keswick, at an old signpost indicating Castlerigg Stone Circle and, in the opposite direction, Walla Crag, the first objective of the day. This is unquestionably one of the easiest of starts, with the amount of effort required being barely sufficient to burn off the guest house 'Full English'.

A leisurely stroll through a series fields gets things under way, to a stile onto the Rakefoot farm road. Take this up towards the farm, forking right at another Walla Crag signpost and onto the open fell-side. A short climb along by a big wall, then through a gate for an airy stroll high above Derwent Water, brings you to the summit at 1234ft. All in all, only some 500ft of climbing. You can now reflect on the minimum amount of energy you have expended to get there; a fine example of gain without pain. Derwent Water and the Coledale fells are especially well seen from this magnificent vantage point, and if you are fortunate enough to have the weather on your side, the watery light of the early morning sun will enhance what is already an idyllic scene.

To the southeast lies the way ahead, onto higher ground and the first pronounced summit on the main ridge, that of Bleaberry Fell. The wide path heads down to a stile, which should be climbed in order to continue along what has become a well-used path which averts the unpleasantness of ploughing through the dense heather which covers large areas of the lower slopes. It is only a mile from Walla Crag but to me it always seems a great deal further. I put this down to the simplicity of the route's beginning, which lulls you into thinking that perhaps the whole day will be as straightforward as the first mile. Walks of this distance never are.

Head left when the path splits to avoid ending up at Ashness Bridge, to maintain your assault on Bleaberry Fell. The day's first wet bits are now underfoot, although you don't need me to tell you this, and the path gradually bears right in an attempt to escape it; unfortunately it never quite succeeds. After a large sheepfold is passed, the going gets better, albeit steeper, for a short and stony climb to the first of three big cairns where the incline lessens considerably.

A short way further on you will reach the largest of the three which marks the highest point of Bleaberry Fell at 1932ft, and also part two of boggy territory stretching southwards. On a typical fell-walk, if such a thing really exists, the second summit of the day is usually considered to be a convenient lunch stop, but today I would strongly advise against reaching for the sandwich box at this stage for there is still a long way to go. It may still indeed be too early for elevenses.

The path now proceeds to take a winding course to the first 'island in the swamp', crossing a fence in reaching the two topped summit of High Seat at 1996ft. One of them is simply named Man and houses a shapely cairn, the other an OS column. Despite the presence of the latter, it is very difficult to distinguish its highest point. Fell views as numerous as any in the district can be appreciated from here, however many miss out as this summit is rarely visited.

On eventually tearing yourself away from this superb viewpoint, head south to yet another stile at a fence corner, to pick up the ridge path bound for High Tove, descending the gradual slope on the left side of the fence which has been erected in a way the Romans would have been proud of. High Seat to High Tove measures a single mile as the crow flies, but once level ground is reached, the path is forced to take a far from direct route, and you with it. You have no choice but to leave the line of the fence more times than I care to remember, in trying desperately to avoid the worst of the horrendous peat bog. A hillwalking friend, whose boots had sadly seen better days was once known to resort to bare feet for this section, whilst taking care to look out for anything the resident amphibious sheep might have left in his path.

At a right angle in the fence, leave it to proceed south, to conclude a good deal more than a mile's walk to High Tove. The solitary summit cairn at 1665ft stands slightly away from a further fence which has taken up the southward line vacated by its predecessor. The length of the Helvellyn ridge across the Thirlmere valley attracts attention from this oasis in a 'desert' of bog.

From High Tove, a few paces regains the ridge path for the long haul to Ullscarf. After bypassing Armboth Fell to the east, the route sticks to the now familiar ridge fence, crossing it where it diverts off to the right, just above Blea Tarn, and over the Wythburn – Watendlath path. You do meet the fence once again, this time to pass through it at a gate for the thin track climbing by the left side of the impressive Standing Crag. The path swings right above its topmost rocks, then heads south in rejoining the fence, to meet up with a line of old fence posts which in turn lead to Ullscarf's sizeable summit cairn across gently rising ground. Time now for lunch and a well earned rest whilst emptying boots and wringing out socks.

The summit of Ullscarf at 2370ft is one where little time is generally spent, on account of the desire to move on to one of the best known of Lakeland's central fells, High Raise, only a couple of miles beyond which offers the added bonus of the first clear sight of the Langdale Pikes. The old posts still prove a valuable southward marker off the extensive top, although wet ground cannot be entirely avoided as the route now aims down past a small tarn to Greenup Edge, the pass linking Far Easedale with Borrowdale.

The climb to High Raise is straightforward on a wide trench worn into the fell-side, passing over its subordinate, Low White Stones, then onto the main fell itself (the summit is known as High White Stones) at exactly 2500ft. High Raise is often thought of as the most central of the Lake District, and is of sufficient altitude to provide magnificent all round views with a multitude of peaks well seen. It is also fitting that it happens to feature in the Ordnance Survey's trigonometrical calculations.

A very easy walk across a high plateau in a southeasterly direction reveals what is only a short scramble to Sergeant Man, certainly not seen at its best from this approach. Thankfully the summit at 2414ft is far from dreary, positioned at the very edge of steep crags which should be borne in mind if enveloped in mist. Sergeant Man is a popular climb and on a fine day you will most likely find yourself in the company of travellers from Grasmere who have continued beyond Easedale Tarn and who are eager to enthuse about their exploits with you over afternoon tea. Who can blame them; it is an excellent place to share some fell-top banter.

Rejoin the main path to continue southeast, to cross the Grasmere – Great Langdale path above Eagle Crag and Blea Crag which both dominate the upper Easedale Tarn valley to gain the extensive summit of Blea Rigg at 1776ft. The fell is adorned with numerous rocky outcrops which can create difficulty in determining its highest point. Continue along the pronounced ridge separating Great Langdale from Easedale and after a varied couple more miles on a winding path, Silver How is reached at the end of a short ascent. As with Walla Crag, very fine views are offered for the minimum of effort. At 1292ft, Silver How is a fashionable climb from Grasmere village, and having walked so far you must try to resist the temptation to make the quick descent in order to frequent one of its fine watering holes, as with nine peaks down, only Loughrigg Fell now remains.

From Silver How, an undulating path can be traced, deviating little from southeast, dropping exasperatingly drops down to the Red Bank road at 500ft. Follow the road up past High Close Youth Hostel, then after a junction, leave the road to the right for the public bridleway at a wall sign for Rydal. Beyond a kissing gate, at the foot of a steep slope you are faced with yet another tempting short cut around Loughrigg Terrace and Rydal Water. Summon up one last show of resilience and determination for such attributes will be needed on this short, and after so many miles, brutal ascent to Loughrigg Fell's 1099ft summit. Loughrigg possesses a labyrinth of paths criss-crossing its sprawling acres so keep an eye in the direction of Ambleside when descending. The main path leads down to a rough road passing Brow Head Farm, crossing the river Rothay by means of a narrow stone bridge, and into Rothay Park. After passing the church the town is eventually reached, completing a very long, very rewarding and very soggy day.

Skiddaw and Keswick from Walla Crag

Route 21: Taking a Hike on Dodds, Peaks and Pikes

Walk File

Distance: 15½ miles.

Total Ascent: 4300ft.

Start: Wanthwaite (GR 316231, OS 2½" map, NE sheet).

Finish: Grasmere.

Terrain: A steep and rough climb to attain the ridge, then on good paths across mostly grassy hills.

Lakeland Maps: OS 1:25000 Outdoor Leisure series NE sheet no. 5 and SE sheet no. 7.

Public Transport: Nothing down St. John's in the Vale to reach start point. Bus service 555 Lancaster & Kendal – Keswick. Stops at St. John's in the Vale/A591 road junction, and also in Grasmere.

Features visited:

Clough Head	2382ft
Great Dodd	2807ft
Watson's Dodd	2584ft
Stybarrow Dodd	2756ft
Raise	2889ft
White Side	2832ft
Helvellyn	3118ft
Helvellyn Lower Man	*3033ft*
Nethermost Pike	2920ft
Dollywaggon Pike	2810ft

If your idea of the ideal hill walk is to be able to stride out all day across a high level ridge of welcoming grassy tops without the problem of negotiating difficult terrain then the eight and a half mile long Helvellyn range which maintains a direct north-south line separating the Thirlmere

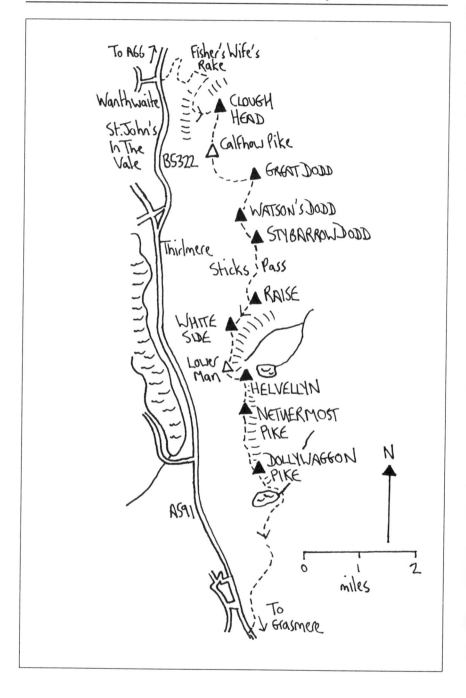

and Patterdale lowlands is most definitely for you. Add a further seven miles to allow for gaining access to and departing from this group of dormant giants and you have a route of the highest order surmounting nine major summits, with only one of them failing to reach the 2500ft contour.

Although without complex terrain, this is a long day and as with all excursions into the high fells, should not be underestimated. A traverse of the complete length of the ridge demands the use of two cars or the Kendal – Keswick service bus, although if the latter option is chosen an extra two miles along the road is necessary from the bus shelter on the A591 at the St. John's In The Vale road junction to reach the start point. The grassy reputation of these fells precedes them, therefore a first sighting of the craggy west face of the first on the ridge, Clough Head, is an unexpected surprise. This rock wall plays a major part in the morning's events.

From Wanthwaite, where there is very limited car parking, follow the wide track signposted to Matterdale, leaving it after a couple of hundred yards at a stile on the right. From the stile, climb up towards the spoil heaps of the disused Hilltop Quarries, where a couple of excavators maintain a ghostly vigil. Turn right along an old vehicle track and past the stacked up sections of old rails once used here. Where a wide grass track begins to climb left, keep to the lower path, still surfaced in places, before leaving this left at a ruined building until almost upon the empty buildings of Bramcrag Quarries. Look out for a tall rusted iron post on your left which is a useful marker for a small gate sitting further up the slope, and the only legitimate gap in the intake wall.

The climbing starts straight away, a tough slog on grass surrounded by encroaching rivers of scree up to the base of the rock wall. The defences of these seemingly impregnable crags towering above are breached by the steep passage of Fisher's Wife's Rake. This is an exhilarating but demanding little scramble which requires careful attention, but once its upper confines are reached there is ample opportunity to replenish your energy reserves for the walk to the fell-top.

From the head of the rake, Clough Head's summit lies directly northeast. Keep to this bearing whereupon you will come across Jim's Fold, a sheepfold of dimensions sufficient to give refuge to we humans as well as our ovine compatriots. There is no real path to speak of across the final slopes, but the going is straightforward if not rather prolonged on firm grass, with ever widening views to the north and west. An OS column and adjoining circular shelter crown the top at 2382ft, the lowest to be visited on this elevated itinerary, but with the highlight of the head on spectacle of the ravaged south face of Blencathra across the Threlkeld valley.

North to Helvellyn Summit (Neil Richardson)

Now begins the crossing of the ridge in earnest, whose friendly gradients make for rapid progress. The initially faint narrow track takes a direct line south on grass interspersed with peaty patches to the isolated rocky eminence of Calfhow Pike, before swinging round sharply eastward towards Great Dodd, needing a detour from the main path which dodges the final climb in the rush to regain the natural line of the watershed. A few rocks have been scraped together by some spirited individuals to line the approach to the summit with several cairns. A lonely pile of stones stands on the grassy dome at 2807ft, but offers only scant protection against the elements; a small well-built shelter does a better job a hundred yards to the east. Great Dodd is a mountain of massive proportions, and can be a tiresome ascent by any route other than the main ridge. Having once and only once taken on and conquered the west flank direct from St John's Vale, I can vouch for the demoralising extent of its endless gradients.

The path becomes quite rutted on the descent in the direction of the grassy spur of Watson's Dodd only a mile distant. A short detour is required to reach its cairn at 2584ft, which stands away from the beaten track as if outcast by its neighbours to the western extremity of what turns out to be a rather spongy plateau. Head back across the soft ground to rejoin the ridge proper. The path passes a tiny tarn before straightening and taking an exciting line, contouring as a narrow ledge above Stanahgill Head. Once this is rounded, the route heads across the wide expanse to meet the next prominent rise at the tiny cairn of Stybarrow Dodd at 2756ft.

The OS column which is shown to be situated aside the path on the 2½″ map turns out to be conspicuous by its absence at the edge of the slope, on which a faint track has in places become a shallow trench for the easy descent to the Sticks Pass. At just over 2400ft, it is also one of the highest of Lakeland's passes, and is well-trodden by throngs of walkers both following and cutting through the high fells. A couple of years ago I was taking a quick break at Sticks when I was amazed to see a man on horseback pass me, taking advantage of the route's bridleway status. Until then, I thought I was the one bagging these fells at a canter.

The slope now facing you marks the start of a noticeable contrast in terrain, which turns progressively rougher on the short climb to Raise. The main cairn at 2889ft sits in the midst of many rock outcrops, from where the views are most extensive. The north facing slopes become the domain of the skier in the winter months, confirmed by the presence of a hut and ski lift on the Ullswater side. With the distance covered thus far, you may find it hard to believe Raise is only just over half-way in terms of tops attained.

The end of the summit dome is soon reached to the southwest, requiring another easy mile's stroll up to White Side at 2832ft. From the east, a further path rises to this commanding viewpoint, contouring the upper slopes of Kepple Cove along the way.

The succession of rocky crests of the Helvellyn escarpment up ahead in the distance make for fascinating viewing and speed the approach to the first of them, the satellite peak of the Lower Man. From the dividing col your first steps into 3000ft territory do not come easily, for the ascent is quite rough on worn ground. From the pile of stones at 3033ft, the gradient is so easy that the whole slope has virtually taken on the appearance of a ridge path on the way to Helvellyn, such is the immense wear and tear this most popular mountain has to endure. By keeping to the exciting edge above Brown Cove the anticipation of your impending arrival at England's third highest peak can be yet further heightened.

Of the higher fells, I have visited Helvellyn's summit more times than any other, and have no doubts many have it at the top of their 'most climbed' list. Whether done as a single peak or one of a number as the high point of this ridge, it never ceases to generate an aura of awesome grandeur with its twin edges which have to be traversed to be fully appreciated.

From the OS column at 3118ft, follow the escarpment past the cross wall shelter and Memorial in the direction of Nethermost Pike. The path is as clear as you could hope for, splitting into three at a sizeable cairn. From right to left, these head for Wythburn church and Grisedale Tarn respectively, therefore a process of elimination leaves you with the leftmost and least used, which should be followed to traverse the flat top to the summit at 2920ft. Continue south to meet up with the Grisedale Tarn path before leaving it almost straight away to gain the day's final peak, that of Dollywaggon Pike at 2810ft at the edge of a short spur jutting out amongst crags.

The drop down to Grisedale Tarn is very steep and the main path which you will again join by way of a short walk southward is severely eroded. I must admit to not caring for this path as a means of ascent, which is obviously a minority view judging by the hordes of ascending walkers I always seem to pass. Now it is (almost) all downhill to Grasmere, your final destination. The main path rounds the tarn on its south side, then from Grisedale Hause descends gradually by Tongue Gill, emerging at the A591 by Mill Bridge. A short road walk is all that remains down to the village, to complete the highest of high level days.

Route 22:
When on High Street . . .

Walk File

Distance: 13¾ miles.

Total Ascent: 2900ft.

Start: Howtown village.

Finish: Queen's Head Hotel, Troutbeck village.

Terrain: Easy going once the ridge is gained. Good paths on generally grassy fells.

Lakeland Maps: OS 1:25000 Outdoor Leisure series NE sheet no. 5 and SE sheet no. 7.

Public Transport: Bus service 108 Penrith – Patterdale. Stops Glenridding. Service 517 Glenridding – Bowness. Stops Troutbeck. Ullswater Motor Yacht Glenridding – Howtown. Mountain Goat Windermere – Glenridding (From Tourist Information Centre).

Features visited:

Bonscale Pike	1718ft
Loadpot Hill	2201ft
Wether Hill	2210ft
High Raise	2634ft
Rampsgill Head	2581ft
High Street	2718ft
Thornthwaite Crag	2569ft

If anyone can stake a claim as creating the first conspicuous footpath across the high Lakeland fells then it has to be the Romans. In seeking protection from potential attack from the Brigantes tribes down in the then forest covered valleys, the legions frequently trod a much easier and direct route over a range of grassy and remote hills which today can be discerned at its clearest between the villages of Troutbeck and Tirril. With forts nearby at Ambleside, and just south of Penrith at Brougham, there can be little doubt this route over the fells linked the two together, a total distance of some twenty-six miles and a long day's march.

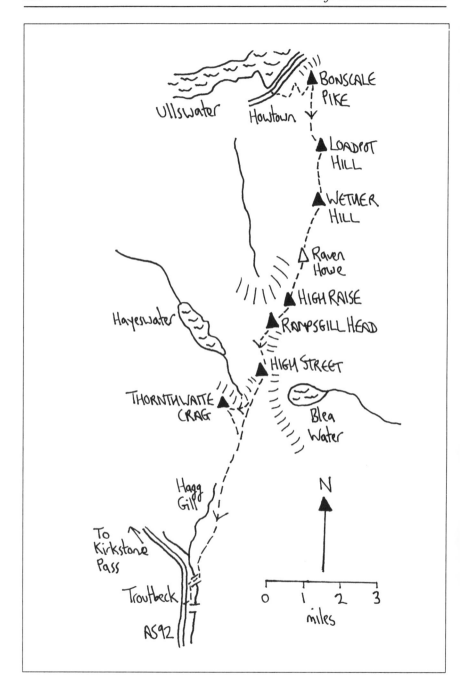

Although the Romans were keen to escape the valleys, they certainly were not enthusiastic peak-baggers, for once up amongst the high ground their priority was to get across this vast tract of exposed territory as swiftly as possible. The lie of the land was most certainly to their advantage, in maintaining a consistently high altitude with little height loss between the gentle contours of the individual fells which make up the ridge. Save for a number of small diversions to reach the summits they chose to bypass, here you have an opportunity to 'do as the Romans did', and follow a section of their famous road.

An enjoyable alternative to arranging a lift round to your start point at Howtown, a small village in a secluded bay on the eastern shore of Ullswater is to take the direct route across the lake on the passenger yacht from Glenridding pier, a journey of thirty-five minutes. From the Howtown landing stage, the land-mass towering above to the east is Bonscale Pike, the subject of the day's first ascent and a fine way onto the main ridge.

Pass the Howtown Hotel on your right to pick up a bridleway to a gate and a four-arrowed signpost. Take the route indicating Pooley Bridge which crosses a beck at a small stone bridge, then heads left past Mellguards to a further gate. This one gives access to the fell-side, where a good track begins to climb straight away by the intake wall, through the dense bracken of the lower slopes. The route swings left, then right at a cairn in order to tackle the western flank's uppermost defences, before eventually emerging into open country. The summit now lies only a short walk away, but a more exhilarating approach to it hugs the edge of the escarpment to the first of two prominent stone towers, both fine airy viewpoints. The second, Bonscale Tower itself, stands further along the edge.

From either tower the summit at 1718ft is easily accessible. From the cairn, with the main ridge now clearly in sight your next steps are to Loadpot Hill, the northernmost of its 2000ft summits. The climb follows intermittent tracks before picking up the Roman Road for the first time, but then leaves it almost immediately to make a bee-line for the OS column at 2201ft. A group of timid fell ponies brave the elements on the slopes of Loadpot Hill, and one or two may decide to take a closer look at you if you seem friendly enough ie you happen to have any food to spare.

You are now faced with the enviable prospect of several miles of easy high level ridge with excellent views whichever way you care to look.

Complete the traverse of Loadpot Hill by heading due south to meet the Roman Road at the now derelict Lowther House (identifiable by 'Chy' on the 2½" OS map). A further leftward diversion across the gently rising slopes of the 2210ft Wether Hill brings the day's third top underfoot. Contour slightly west of south to regain the course of the Road, where after a short distance the path swings left at a semi-collapsed wall, then proceeds through a gap in it. As the smooth gradients of these fells offer scant protection from the weather, the wall comes highly recommended as a useful wind-free back-rest for a lunch stop.

The ridge now begins to rise gradually, but more significantly in the shape of High Raise, second only to the still elusive High Street in terms of altitude. A fence soon joins the route on the right, then a wall on the left in traversing the secondary top of Raven Howe. Excellent westward views can be had, including a fine foreground of the Rampsgill valley sweeping round beneath Rest Dodd and The Nab. The path trends right to thread its way through the fence, then passes back through it at a corner to complete the ascent across unobstacled fell-side. The now customary leftward deviation will take you across High Raise's stony top to its small cairn at 2634ft and nearby summit shelter.

The descent and re-ascent necessary to attain the peak at the head of the Rampsgill valley is hardly noticeable. The more interesting of a choice of routes is to pick up the track which keeps near the edge of its rough upper slopes on its approach to a two cairned top, the highest at 2581ft. The location for the other was an inspired choice, displaying the length of Rampsgill and a lot more besides.

All that now stands between you and the day's highest and best known ground is the marked col of the Straits of Riggindale. Continue a southwestward course to reach the depression before leaving the Roman Road to take its course below the summit across the western flank for the next mile, whilst you undertake the day's last climb of any note. The path strikes up the narrow but easy northern slope by the left side of High Street's substantial wall.

I recall one February day when two of us had set out from Hartsop intending a high level circuit of Hayeswater. Conditions were dull and windy, but the cloud was off the fells and the snow-line was soon encountered. The weather began to deteriorate just as we reached High Street's OS column, which made our minds up for us to turn back. Towards the Riggindale col and soon enveloped in a near white-out, my companion was walking alongside me at around arm's length yet I was having difficulty seeing and hearing him. With the blizzard raging, I soon felt very rough ground which prompted me to stop dead. I thought this unusual as the snow was very deep and tightly packed, and furthermore I knew that beneath the snow the hill was grassy. At this point the wind eased and I could then see the ground; I could not believe I had actually stumbled onto the summit wall at one of its lower sections where the drifting snow had almost completely covered it. It is worth keeping directional walls close by in bad conditions but this close?

Before long, the incline levels out into High Street's vast top. An OS column stands close to the wall, the highest point at 2718ft. The 2½" OS map shows the High Street plateau as Racecourse Hill, so named as in the early 19th century the summit was the location for an annual horse racing meeting. This must have been quite an event.

Although it lies at the apex of the famous Kentmere Horseshoe round, the summit of High Street is slightly set back from its fells which steeply enclose the upper Kentmere valley to the south, which as a consequence are much better seen from elsewhere. Despite this, even from a summit so extensive much fine mountain scenery can be appreciated in other directions.

Looking South from Thornthwaite Crag

Depart the OS column southwards. When the accompanying wall turns away to the right, proceed across the open fell-side to follow the wide path bearing right above the Hayeswater valley to the fine tower of stones which crowns the summit of Thornthwaite Crag at 2569ft. With another sturdy wall as shelter, this is a good situation for afternoon tea before starting out on the long descent to Troutbeck village.

The route continues south from the cairn as though heading for Froswick, the next peak on the horseshoe, but before it does join the path branching off to the right (the next section of the Roman Road) for a lengthy traverse into the valley. The track slants down on grass through bracken on its descent, and where more level ground is reached, follows Hagg Gill and passes between the Froswick/Ill Bell/Yoke ridge and the more diminutive Troutbeck Tongue to the right. Do not take the bridle-way, signposted at a gate across the path, but continue straight ahead, whereupon the path swings right down to another gate and signpost indicating the way through the fields of Troutbeck Park Farm to a fine solitary tree by Hagg Bridge.

The route now picks up the farm road for a pleasant final mile's stroll, via Ing Bridge and Ing Lane before climbing steadily up through the houses of Troutbeck village for a hopefully timely arrival at the Queen's Head by the A592. What better place to finish.

Route 23:
Blencathra and Beyond

Walk File

Distance: 10 miles.

Total Ascent: 2900ft.

Start/Finish: Mungrisdale village.

Terrain: Fair paths/tracks on generally featureless hills (Blencathra excepted), with an exposed rocky scramble (Sharp Edge) in between.

Lakeland Maps: OS 1:50000 Landranger series Sheet 90 Penrith & Keswick.

Public Transport: Nothing which is convenient. Bus service X5 Keswick – Penrith, nearest stop is the A66 at Mungrisdale road end.

Features visited:

Souther Fell	1713ft
Blencathra	2847ft
Bannerdale Crags	2241ft
Bowscale Fell	2306ft

The considerable number of routes taking full advantage of every aspect of Blencathra's spectacular mountain topography make it a highly sought after expedition in itself. To visit a lone summit, even if that did happen to be Blencathra, usually denies the hillwalker the pleasure of following a ridge or two, therefore as a variation on simply tackling this fine peak as the day's one and only objective it can be neatly slotted into a useful circuit comprising three of its eastern neighbours, close by but hugely unwalked by comparison.

The start point is Mungrisdale village some three miles off the main A66 between Keswick and Penrith. Ample parking can be found in a small area by the River Glenderamackin just below the Mill Inn. From the car park, a small footbridge spans the river for the Inn and also the narrow road around the base of the fells to Scales. As the stile in the top

corner of the field immediately behind the Inn is now regrettably blocked
off to hillwalkers, the shortest route to attain the day's first ridge has to
be ignored and replaced by a short walk along the road in the direction
of Scales to the point where it is gated. Here you can strike up the slope
through bracken to traverse the open fell immediately above the intake
wall back to the aforementioned blocked stile. Now you are on its correct
side, you can commence the climb of Souther Fell with a clear conscience.

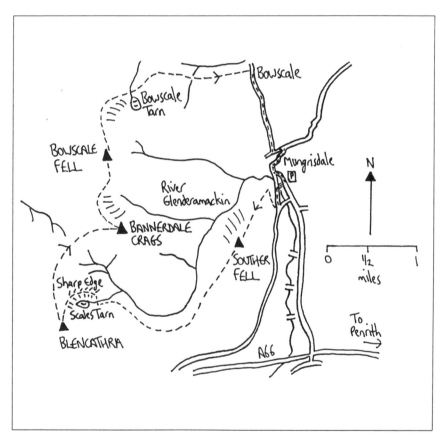

A long strip of worn grass makes a useful path amongst the bracken
cloaked lower slopes, making light of the gradient. An ocean of grass
soon provides some relief for the latter stages of the approach to the
tiniest of summit cairns at 1713ft, which will only leave you speculating
as to the source of its few stones. Continue southwest along the length

of the summit ridge to a considerably larger cairn which would undoubtedly be more at home taking pride of place on Souther Fell's summit. Nevertheless, it still commands a fine location at the head of the flank looking towards Blencathra's famous saddle.

An easy descent now follows to the col at Mousethwaite Combe, to pick up the blazed trail from Scales. You are now well and truly *en route* for Sharp Edge, and the gentle traverse of the lower slopes of Scales Fell only serves to enhance the sense of anticipation you will be feeling. When the route swings left to climb more steeply, cross the tumbling Scales Beck up to the dark and brooding waters of its beautiful tarn, from where a first glimpse of Sharp Edge's serrated profile may start those butterflies fluttering. As you would expect, the path up to the start of the Edge is very worn, merging unannounced into this most awe-inspiring of corrie rims for an exhilarating half hour's expedition. My palms are sweating just typing these lines.

Sharp Edge is inevitably compared with Helvellyn's Striding Edge to determine which of them is the best. I am of the view that to relegate one to second place is a grossly unjust thing to do, for each should be appreciated on its own merits. I have heard it said that your favourite mountain is the one you happen to be standing on at the time; this statement holds good for each of these two renowned mountain aretes. You will no doubt agree that Sharp Edge is aptly named as you scramble over and around the numerous outcrops and pinnacles high above Scales Tarn's black pool. A path skirts the top rocks a few feet down to the right which does prove a useful escape from the crest, for in some places the exposure can be quite stomach-turning, in particular one notorious step above an airy void to gain so called safer ground.

Once the arete has been successfully negotiated, a steep scramble not dissimilar to that which immediately follows Striding Edge is then required. So many have come this way before it is now a matter of selecting your own way up the vastly eroded incline to reach more level ground for the easy 'saddle' traverse above the impressive bowl of crags which fall away to Scales Tarn, over to Blencathra's summit at 2847ft. The ground immediately south of the main cairn falls away suddenly in forming another excellent route of ascent, namely the Halls Fell ridge, and as a consequence leaves a vast uninterrupted panorama towards Lakeland's very heart.

The way ahead narrowly avoids the retracing of steps by taking a line directly north across the centre of the grassy saddle as opposed to that

On Sharp Edge (by Mark Walsh)

just taken. The walking is very easy and pleasant, passing a small pool which in somebody's book may pass for a tarn, two very conspicuous white stone crosses, and numerous directional cairns leading almost to the top of Foule Crag before bending slightly left for a short rocky descent. The rough terrain soon dissipates into grassy expanses through which a reasonable track runs, down to a depression separating Blencathra from your next target, Bannerdale Crags, and the commencement of more remote territory.

It is worth remembering a safe way down to the Glenderamackin valley can be found here, however your route lies across the 'pass', in following a clear track sweeping eastward across the grassy flank. This becomes surprisingly less distinct as the contour lines spread out during the final yards of the approach to the small pile of stones at the highest point at 2241ft. Here is yet another supreme summit location, being only a matter of feet from the sweeping arc of crags after which the hill is named and, being an eastern outlier, a good viewing station for the high Pennines.

The next few minutes walk calls for sure-footedness as you pick up the good path which faithfully maintains the closest line possible excitingly above the craggy headwall of the upper Bannerdale valley. The grassy dome of Bowscale Fell is the last of the day's quartet to be visited, but not via this escarpment-clinging track. When the fell is clearly in view in the distance leave it to make your way up to the left, through a marshy patch to meet a further track which is most eerie in its origins, springing up from seemingly nowhere in particular in the midst of the grassy tract.

The mysterious path strikes a direct course for the summit, first reaching a large stone shelter, with the cairn a hundred yards distant. At 2306ft, Bowscale Fell is one of the larger of the group, and represents a beacon over the most magnificent wild country, with Bannerdale Crags particularly good from this angle. Concentrate your gaze northward and it is very easy to momentarily forget you are in Lakeland, such is the beautifully featureless terrain coupled with an absence of fellow walkers. The other way reveals a distinctive undulating skyline of better known peaks in the distance.

You would be forgiven for assuming the ground to the north comprises nothing but expansive grassy slopes. Leave the summit in this direction and you will shortly discover this is not so. By avoiding the east ridge in bearing slightly left across the grassy level to the edge of Tarn Crags, Bowscale Tarn comes into view far below set in an impressive rocky amphitheatre. Continue north to follow this edge down for a short way until you meet up with the faintest of tracks heading east towards the corrie, to drop down to the outflow of the tarn on what is a good zigzag path between its craggy defences.

Two of us were descending this grassy rake recently when a boot slipped and dislodged a small rock on the path. Two sheep were contentedly chewing the grass below and well to the left of us, so as the rock bounded on down the slope we were confident it would easily miss them. Just as we were about to breathe sighs of relief the rock changed course of its own free will and started leftward towards the grazing pair, under the guise of some heat-seeking missile, and to our horror proceeded to strike one of them full on the rear quarters. As the two very soon continued their munching, we concluded with relief that mercifully no serious damage had been done, sore rump notwithstanding.

With moraines enclosing it almost completely on all sides, Bowscale Tarn is one of Lakeland's finest but nowadays least visited examples of a corrie tarn. Here is an excellent feature to discover on the latter stages of the day's route, and just when you thought you had had your day's quota of geology at its finest. An ever improving path leaves the tarn's outflow and contours the northern slope of the fell, eventually terminating at Bowscale hamlet on a sharp bend of the Hesket Newmarket – Mungrisdale road. An easy last mile along the road will complete an eventful day in returning you to your start point at the Mill Inn.

Route 24:
Breaking New Ground behind The Northern Giants

Walk File

Distance: 12½ miles.

Total Ascent: 2850ft.

Start/Finish: Mosedale, Mungrisdale – Hesket Newmarket road.

Terrain: Very little rough ground. Good walking on mostly good paths/tracks, with some marsh *en route*.

Lakeland Maps: OS 1:50000 Landranger series Sheet 90 Penrith & Keswick.

Public Transport: Nothing which is convenient. Bus service X5 Keswick – Penrith, nearest stop is the A66 at Mungrisdale road end.

Features visited:

Carrock Fell	2174ft
High Pike	2159ft
Knott	2329ft
Great Calva	2265ft

If you're ever asked to name any of the fells which comprise the land mass which lies beyond the A66 to the northeast of Keswick, do not be surprised if the list you come up with happens to be short. The blame for this is likely to be the fault of the two highest peaks of the area, namely Skiddaw and Blencathra which readily spring to mind, and which together tend to monopolise explorations. Beyond these two giants and for the most part obscured from view from the south save for the sneak preview through the 'great central rift', is a group of seemingly rather innocuous hills. Nothing could be further from the truth.

The collective identification of this group as merely the fells 'Back O'Skidda' has no doubt deflected attention elsewhere thus helping to

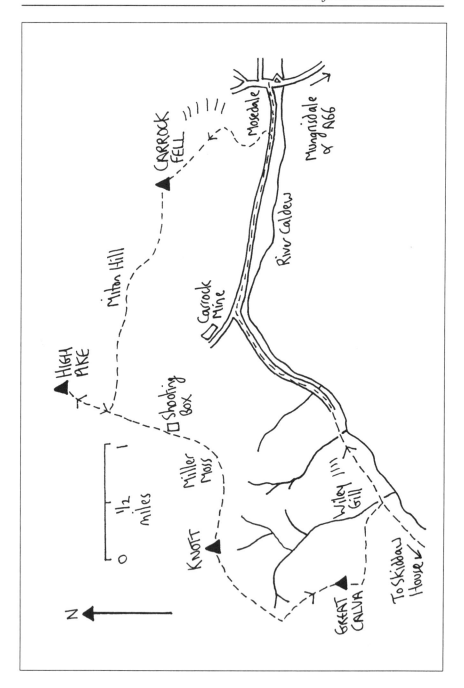

preserve as new, a walking area of great quality. Here is mile after mile of magnificent remote wild country wandering where walkers seldom venture, therefore if you are looking for a real 'get away from it all' day then a journey into the very heart of this unfrequented group is definitely for you.

One such expedition begins from the hamlet of Mosedale, which is situated about four miles along the Mungrisdale road from its junction at the main A66. Parking here is extremely limited. The day's walking starts by following the Carrock Mine road which is signposted for Swineside. At a wall corner, look out for the fell-side track on the right which offers a most interesting climb, snaking its way through the rocks and stones which litter the lower slopes of Carrock Fell's southern flank. As you gain height, heather replaces the stony mass which does make for easier going, but only marginally due to the continued presence of more awkward boulders. As the contours begin to spread out, the track rises to the remnants of what once must have been a quite sizeable sheepfold. From the fold, the summit falls easily, only necessitating a simple walk.

At 2174ft, Carrock Fell is easily overtopped by several other fells in the immediate vicinity, but is in a different league as regards originality, a most thought provoking summit. First and foremost, your gaze will inevitably fix on the strange near-complete ring of stones which encircles the main cairn. This is believed to be the ruin of a Celtic hill fort of the Brigantine tribe who are understood to have ruled the area until Roman occupation.

Geographically the summit is very much a one-off, at least as far as this particular area is concerned, being composed of volcanic rock quite untypical of the neighbouring grassy slopes which cover Skiddaw Slates. More remarkable is the fact that Gabbro (the rock of the Skye Cuillin) can also be found here. With all this to look at, make sure you do not find yourself distracted from what is a fine view, in which numerous high fells are visible in a southern sweep. Being only a couple of miles within the National Park perimeter, this rocky outpost also reveals a fine Pennine backcloth to the east.

A two-mile ridge more akin to a broad tract of upland moor stretches out to the northwest with at the end of it, your next peak, High Pike. The rocky environs are very soon left behind as marshy territory attempts to disrupt what is generally comfortable progress on grass. Continue over the grassy dome of Miton Hill with your goal ever closer. The track rounds the upper slopes of the old Driggith Mine valley in a marked change of direction to the northeast, joining a route which skirts the summit itself in its quick dash to reach lower ground. You will therefore need to make a short detour to ascend the final 200ft to High Pike's broad top. What this fell lacks in difficult terrain it makes up for with what is another intriguing summit boasting a number of features.

The summit of High Pike

A short line of stones which serves as a useful shelter links the 2159ft OS column and a massive cairn, behind which sits a memorial seat constructed from slate slabs. No need to spend time searching round for a flat rock to sit on up here; the seat provides a most convenient lunch stop to appreciate the far reaching prospect northward towards Solway and Border country. A short walk in this direction from the seat will bring you to a second stone shelter, this one being the ruin of a shepherd's cottage which even by the standards of today's developers would surely be considered too far gone to be ripe for conversion – wouldn't it?

The retracing of steps, the bane of the hillwalker, takes thankfully only a few minutes as the main path is rejoined. This time it is to be followed southwest across the well-drained grassy gradients of Great Lingy Hill

to its shooting box, which is clearly shown, but un-named on the 1¼"
OS map. This solidly built structure offers welcome escape from the
winds which sweep these featureless fells. Such was the strength of the
gale on one visit that I only just managed to gain access with the wind
continually foiling my determined attempts to get the door open.

The shooting box is well seen from nearby fells and stands proudly at
the head of the Grainsgill valley which has Carrock Mine nestling in its
lower reaches. The mine is believed to have started production in the mid
1850s. Although a number of minerals were extracted, the important
discovery of rich veins of wolfram (tungsten) was its claim to fame, a
metal not extracted elsewhere in the district. Extensive working took
place for several years until market forces turned against the product at
the end of The Great War, sounding the death knell for its continued
existence as a viable proposition and leading to closure only a year later
in 1919.

Cross the expansive marsh of Miller Moss at Grainsgill Beck. The path
next swings westward and almost peters out as though wishing to be
excused from making the rather tedious climb to attain Knott's extensive
summit at 2329ft. This is the highest point reached on the round, the
grassiest and it must be said, the dullest of the day's quartet. Nevertheless, several well-known names can just be picked out in the far distance.
A somewhat shorter circuit takes the good line of descent from Knott
over its eastern shoulder Coomb Height, eventually returning you to the
Carrock Mine road and back to Mosedale, but in doing so would omit
an interesting continuation towards the cone shaped Great Calva which
is not to be missed.

A now better defined track trends southwest dispelling any thoughts
of a bee-line to Calva, and drops quickly to a small col. The ensuing climb
of some 500ft is quite steep in places and accompanies an old fence on
spongy ground to a startling looking cairn of mangled iron posts jammed
between rocks, marking the summit at 2265ft. Equally good if not better
viewing can be had from the south cairn where the immensity of Skiddaw can be fully appreciated, with its upland 'forest' well seen in the
foreground. Nestling in amongst a small huddle of protecting trees is
Skiddaw House, once a shepherd's cottage but now the wildest of
locations for a Youth Hostel. With this as your base you can increase your
knowledge of and affection for these retiring hills.

The temptation now is to maintain a southerly line and aim for
Skiddaw House itself, but the required route of descent is one which lies

to the east, just before the south cairn. The course of the old fence, built to enclose the forest, is as good as any, therefore keep it close by through the dense heather on the descent to more level ground at the bridge by the Wiley Gill sheepfold. You are now on the well used Skiddaw House – Mosedale path which offers a long but enjoyable passage out through this lonely territory.

As all four fells so far climbed lie to the north and west of the River Caldew, there is a temptation to include one on its opposite bank. The nearest to Calva is the sprawling mass of Mungrisdale Common, certainly the most uninspiring of the Lake District's 2000ft fells, and its inclusion in Wainwright's Northern Fells guidebook no doubt has something to do with the fact anyone ever sets foot on it at all. Do it if you like, but I will assure you it won't be on my account.

Passing tantalisingly close to Bannerdale Crags and Bowscale Fell, the good path keeps to the north side of the river following the base of the ridge you have just traversed. Just beyond the Carrock Mine buildings, a couple of quick tarmac miles ends the day's events back at Mosedale, a day away from the masses in the company of one of the district's most secretive regions.

Route 25: The 'Seven Threes'

Walk File

Distance: 47 miles.

Total Ascent: 10250ft.

Start/Finish: Keswick Moot Hall.

Terrain: Good paths on ground ranging from smooth grassy tops to the boulder fields of the Scafells.

Lakeland Maps: OS 1:25000 Outdoor Leisure series NW sheet no.4, NE sheet no. 5 & SW sheet no. 6.

Public Transport: Bus service 555 Kendal – Keswick. Service X5 Whitehaven – Keswick.

Features visited:

Skiddaw	3054ft
Scafell	3162ft
Scafell Pike	3210ft
Broad Crag	*3054ft*
Ill Crag	*3040ft*
High Raise	2500ft
Helvellyn	3118ft
Helvellyn Lower Man	*3033ft*

Sadly England possesses little ground which exceeds the magical 3000ft contour, and what there is can be found conveniently within the Lake District National Park represented by Skiddaw, Helvellyn and the Scafells. The four are so dispersed as to be neither too close together nor too far apart and as such a continuous journey on foot linking them presents a tempting and stretching challenge. Add a twenty-four-hour time constraint for completion of the route and you have a double-edged test of mental and physical resolve. In addition to the four well-known summits there are a further three satellite peaks in close proximity which can rightly join their company as they too protrude above 3000ft. These additional tops are clearly defined, but not to the extent that they could

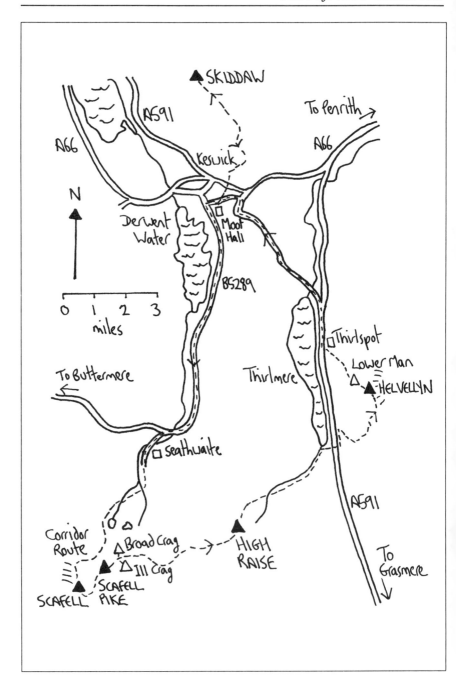

ever be classed as mountains in their own right. Due to the distance involved maximum daylight hours are essential, therefore four weeks either side of the longest day is the best time of year, giving approximately eighteen hours of daylight. I would recommend a start time of 2am, making a night ascent of the first of the seven 'threes', Skiddaw, to experience the spectacle of sunrise from its summit.

Fitness is a pre-requisite for such an undertaking. If you've covered the previous twenty-four routes in this volume you'll certainly be in good shape for this forty-seven miler. As some fifteen of them are on road in linking the main mountain groupings, you may feel the faithful boots may be too cumbersome. If you do, quality fell trainers are a good substitute.

Skiddaw is climbed by the much maligned tourist path from Keswick Moot Hall in the market square. From the square, pass through Fitz Park by the cricket pavilion to join the course of the old railway. A short way along, leave it on the right down a little slope, then head up the road turning left onto Spooney Green Lane and on around the base of Latrigg to Gale Road End. Take the muddy track between wall and fence which leads onto the open fell-side past the monument, climbing steeply past Jenkin Hill. The ground then levels out into a well worn path flanking Skiddaw Little Man, and on to Skiddaw itself. The path contours expertly high above Skiddaw Forest before swinging left on loose stony terrain to attain the lengthy and inevitably wind lashed summit ridge. All of it has to be traversed in order to reach the OS column at its north end at 3054ft, from where dawn will (hopefully) reveal a conglomeration of peaks backing Derwent Water. Among them are the Scafells, your next port of call. With your first peak under your belt, retrace your steps to Keswick, whereupon you will have completed approximately a quarter of the climbing and a quarter of the mileage. All this and still no sign of the milkman.

The next section of around nine miles leads through the picturesque Borrowdale valley. With the early morning sun percolating through the rising mists and cocks crowing in the nearby farms contributing to a euphoric state of mind, it is very tempting to try and pick up the pace to get ahead of schedule. Conserve your energy for the mountain sections, where it will be most needed. Towards the end of the Borrowdale valley where the B5289 turns sharp right to begin the climb over the Honister Pass, continue straight on down the narrow road to Seathwaite Farm, reputedly England's wettest inhabited place.

Press on between the farm buildings to join the wide path to Stockley Bridge astride the crystal clear waters of Grains Gill. Cross the tiny bridge to follow a skilfully constructed path of inlaid rocks and stones. After a brief climb the incline eases to almost un-noticeable on the approach to Sty Head Tarn, next to which a tent or two can usually be found away from the busy Borrowdale camp-sites below.

Pick up the path heading southward, traversing the flanks of Great End and Scafell Pike. This is the famous Corridor Route, one of the classic entrances into the Scafells, skirting the top of the dramatic gash of Piers Gill before surmounting Lingmell Col. Beyond the col the path crosses the rocky terrain of Hollow Stones below the menacing buttress of Scafell Crag.

From the foot of the cliff, enter the narrow enclosed ravine of Lords Rake. This is easy scrambling territory par excellence. The ground is very eroded and flakes of the rock wall have a tendency to come away in your hand at vital moments of gaining a decent hold. The first respite from the slope is a tiny col, from where you turn sharp left into the vast chasm of Deep Ghyll to pick up the West Wall Traverse. A scintillating ascent brings you out on the summit plateau leaving only a stroll over to Scafell's cairn at 3162ft.

A degree of doubling back on yourself is now called for to gain Scafell Pike. To avoid descending the same way, head east on a good path to Foxes Tarn, which takes you in the direction of Eskdale and involves a small climb back to the Mickledore col. The final climb to the peak across a massive boulder field is arduous at the best of times, but adrenalin will more than compensate for any fatigue.

England's highest ground warrants an extended rest period, for it is not often you get the opportunity to be the highest person in the country at 3210ft. You may even arrive early enough to be able to climb the few steps of the huge summit cairn and stand alone at this privileged place. Neighbouring fells seem to bow in deference from this superior view-point. The eerie silence of the early morning should be savoured at leisure, in the knowledge that in two or three hours time the place will be teeming with life after you have long since departed.

Leave the summit to the northeast, descending steeply to Broad Crag Col. You will now need to indulge in a spot of peak bagging to pick off Broad Crag and Ill Crag, measuring 3054ft and 3040ft respectively. Fortunately they both lie close to the main route and are easily reached by very short diversions. After following the cairns which mark the way through the boulders, the path becomes more distinct. The descent is gradual and makes for fast going, bypassing Great End and on down to the wall shelter at Esk Hause with close on twenty-eight miles and seven thousand feet of climbing done.

Scafell and Mickledore from Scafell Pike

The route maintains an easterly direction down to Angle Tarn, where the path splits. Take the left branch, skirting the summit of Rossett Pike on to the Stake Pass. The mass of High Raise intervenes unwelcomingly to necessitate a soul destroying ascent, avoidable only by a very wide detour. Grit your teeth and before you know it you will be over its 2500ft summit and striding down its north ridge to Greenup Edge.

The upper Wythburn valley is extremely marshy, and contains a large area known as The Bog, clearly indicated on the OS map. Keep to the path to avoid the worst of the morass which accompanies the Wyth Burn down to Steel End farm at the southern end of Thirlmere. To avoid a dodgy section of road walking, take the signposted forest path on the other side of the A591 to Wythburn church, which now stands alone after the level of the reservoir was increased, claiming its village. As the roadside signpost indicates, three miles to Helvellyn Top await. The presence of any day walkers just starting out will spur you on up the well-used path, as you can measure your progress by their fresh pace.

Before long, you will arrive at the wall shelter, a busy place, and you will be fortunate indeed if a seating space is free. If you mention you've walked thirty-eight miles to get there, someone may relinquish their patch, but at the same time might enquire as to the accuracy of your navigational skills (he can't have walked from Lancaster, can he?).

The OS column stands at 3118ft a short walk beyond the shelter, above the sheer wall of the corrie containing Red Tarn. Continue above the rim of Brown Cove to reach the seventh and smallest of the 'threes', namely Helvellyn Lower Man at 3033ft, before descending northwestwards to the King's Head Inn at Thirlspot. With all the mountain terrain now behind you, a draining six miles on unyielding tarmac remains back to Keswick, when the tiniest of aches and niggles start to manifest themselves in a grandiose manner. You would never be able to live with yourself if you succumbed to thumbing a lift at this late stage, so do not even consider it.

Having said this, I assure you the two hours on the road will pass quickly. In the best traditions of fell endurance events, muster up one last effort to sprint the last few yards to the Moot Hall and on to a nearby hostelry to relive the day's events and perhaps something to numb the pain.

Index of Features Visited

Notes

Every care has been taken in the preparation of this guidebook. However, if you find that any changes have occurred, please record them here and send a copy to Sigma Leisure so that we can update the book for the benefit of other readers:

Notes

Notes

Notes

More Pub Walks . . .

There are many more titles in our fabulous series of 'Pub Walks' books for just about every popular walking area in the UK, all featuring access by public transport. Some of these are listed below – we label our more recent ones as 'best' to differentiate them from inferior competitors! Here is a small selection:

BEST PUB WALKS AROUND CHESTER & THE DEE VALLEY – John Haywood *(£6.95)*

BEST PUB WALKS IN GWENT – Les Lumsdon *(£6.95)*

BEST PUB WALKS IN THE LAKE DISTRICT – Neil Coates *(£6.95)*

PUB WALKS IN SNOWDONIA – Laurence Main *(£6.95)*

PUB WALKS IN POWYS – Les Lumsdon & Chris Rushton *(£6.95)*

BEST PUB WALKS IN PEMBROKESHIRE – Laurence Main *(£6.95)*

BEST PUB WALKS AROUND CENTRAL LONDON – Ruth Herman *(£6.95)*

BEST PUB WALKS IN ESSEX – Derek Keeble *(£6.95)*

Country walking:

THE LAKELAND SUMMITS – Tim Synge *(£7.95)*

100 LAKE DISTRICT HILL WALKS – Gordon Brown *(£7.95)*

LAKELAND ROCKY RAMBLES: Geology beneath your feet – Brian Lynas *(£7.95)*

LAKELAND WALKING, ON THE LEVEL – Norman Buckley *(£6.95)*

MOSTLY DOWNHILL: LEISURELY WALKS, LAKE DISTRICT – Alan Pears *(£6.95)*

CHALLENGING WALKS: NW England & N Wales – Ron Astley *(£7.95)*

FIFTY CLASSIC WALKS IN THE PENNINES – Terry Marsh *(£8.95)*

HILL WALKS IN MID WALES – Dave Ing *(£8.95)*

WEST PENNINE WALKS – Mike Cresswell *(£5.95)*

WELSH WALKS: Dolgellau /Cambrian Coast – L. Main & M. Perrott *(£5.95)*

WELSH WALKS: Aberystwyth & District – L. Main & M. Perrott *(£5.95)*

WALKS IN MYSTERIOUS WALES – Laurence Main *(£7.95)*

RAMBLES IN NORTH WALES – Roger Redfern *(£6.95)*

RAMBLES AROUND MANCHESTER – Mike Cresswell *(£5.95)*

EAST CHESHIRE WALKS – Graham Beech *(£5.95)*

LONDON BUS-TOP TOURIST – John Wittich *(£6.95)*

TEA SHOP WALKS IN THE CHILTERNS – Jean Patefield *(£6.95)*
BY-WAY TRAVELS SOUTH OF LONDON – Geoff Marshall *(£6.95)*

Cycling too!

CYCLE UK! The essential guide to leisure cycling – Les Lumsdon *(£9.95)*
OFF-BEAT CYCLING IN THE PEAK DISTRICT – Clive Smith *(£6.95)*
MORE OFF-BEAT CYCLING IN THE PEAK DISTRICT – Clive Smith *(£6.95)*
50 BEST CYCLE RIDES IN CHESHIRE – edited by Graham Beech *(£7.95)*
CYCLING IN THE COTSWOLDS – Stephen Hill *(£6.95)*
CYCLING IN THE CHILTERNS – Henry Tindell *(£7.95)*
CYCLING IN THE LAKE DISTRICT – John Wood *(£7.95)*
CYCLING IN LINCOLNSHIRE – Penny & Bill Howe *(£7.95)*
CYCLING IN STAFFORDSHIRE – Linda Wain *(£7.95)*
CYCLING IN THE WEST COUNTRY – Helen Stephenson *(£7.95)*
CYCLING IN SOUTH WALES – Rosemary Evans *(£7.95)*
CYCLING IN SCOTLAND & N.E.ENGLAND – Philip Routledge *(£7.95)* .
CYCLING IN NORTH WALES – Philip Routledge *(£7.95)* ... *available 1996*

Sport . . .

THE GOLF COURSES OF CHESHIRE – Mark Rowlinson *(£9.95)*
RED FEVER: from Rochdale to Rio as 'United' supporters – Steve Donoghue *(£7.95)*
UNITED WE STOOD: unofficial history of the Ferguson years – Richard Kurt *(£6.95)*
MANCHESTER CITY: Moments to Remember – John Creighton *(£9.95)*

- plus many more entertaining and educational books being regularly added to our list.
All of our books are available from your local bookshop. In case of difficulty, or to obtain our complete catalogue, please contact:

Sigma Leisure, 1 South Oak Lane, Wilmslow, Cheshire SK9 6AR
Phone: 01625 – 531035   Fax: 01625 – 536800

ACCESS and VISA orders welcome – call our friendly sales staff or use our 24 hour Answerphone service! Most orders are despatched on the day we receive your order – you could be enjoying our books in just a couple of days. Please add £2 p&p to all orders.